SOCIAL MEDIA GPS

A PRACTICAL GUIDE TO
FACEBOOK, TWITTER,
YOUTUBE, LINKEDIN, AND PINTEREST
FOR THE SMALL BUSINESS OWNER

Written & Compiled by

Rachel Bjerstedt & Olivia Myles

© 2011 Marketplace Maven, Allen, TX

TABLE OF CONTENTS

Introduction

This book is meant to be interactive. That means that, in order for this to be useful to you, you MUST participate in the exercises. Yes, that means you'll need to WRITE IN this book! Writing in a book can seem a bit daunting to some. I've been guilty of staring at a blank page for minutes on-end - scared to take the first step and start writing. Because of that, I've made this easy. Stop right here and *scribble* in the box below:

```
Scribble Here
```

See, that wasn't so hard! You've already written in this book, so every last exercise should be completed as well. (Hint: Actually completing the exercises will benefit you and your business in the long-run. So, get going!)

"Contributors" to This Book

If you perform a Google or Bing search for "Social Media Marketing," you will return thousands of results. There's a large community of social media experts and gurus. Many of these experts have similar thoughts, opinions, and theories as to how one should utilize social media.

We have done our best to compile, write, and translate these theories so that they are applicable to YOU – the local/small business owner. Remember something: It takes an entirely different strategy to successfully use social media if your role is owner of "Local Bob's Plumbing" than if your role is CMO of WorldWide Widgets, Inc. So don't get discouraged if you don't have as many friends, fans, followers, or likes, as Widgets, Inc. After all, Widgets, Inc., has different resources and target markets. They more than likely have a team of 25 people who execute and operate their social media strategy. You have only *you* (Well... *maybe* a couple others, if you're lucky).

However, if you're looking for more advanced sources, check out some of our favorites below:

http://www.chrisbrogan.com

http://business.twitter.com

http://ConvinceandConvert.com

http://HubSpot.com

http://MariSmith.com

http://DannyBrown.me

What is Social Media Anyway?

"Social Media" is a simply a fancy phrase that describes the millions and millions of conversations that are supported by online tools.

> **Wikipedia:** *Social Media is media designed to be disseminated through social interaction, created using highly accessible and scalable publishing techniques. Social media uses Internet and web-based technologies to transform broadcast media monologues (one-to-many) into social media dialogues (many-to-many).*

What Social Media Marketing is NOT!

- A cute-looking website with social media buttons/links
- An individual profile on Facebook, Twitter, etc.
- A solo fan/business (branded) page on Facebook
- A registered blog on WordPress, Blogger
- A couple of videos on YouTube, Vimeo, MetaCafé

Your Goal is to Market to Him.

Because He tells two people.
And they tell two people...
and They tell two more people...
... And So On.

Social media marketing is the integration of ALL of these components. In the same way that a chocolate chip cookie is not just a cup of flour and sugar, or an egg or some chocolate chips.

Social Media Tools You Should Know

Traditionally **Blogs** (a contraction of the term "weblog") are a type of website, usually maintained by an individual with regular entries of commentary, descriptions of events, or other material such as graphics or video. (i.e. Blogger, LiveJournal, TypePad, WordPress, etc.)

Micro-blogging is a form of multimedia blogging that allows users to send brief text updates or micro media (such as photos or audio clips) and publish them, either to be viewed by anyone or by a restricted group which can be chosen by the user. A variety of means, including text messaging, instant messaging, e-mail, digital audio or the web can submit these messages. (i.e. Twitter, Plurk, Tumblr, etc.)

Social networking focuses on building online communities of people who share interests and/or activities, or who are interested in exploring the interests and activities of others. Most social network services are web-based and provide a variety of ways for users to interact, such as e-mail and instant messaging services.(i.e. Facebook, LinkedIn, MySpace, Ning, etc.).

Why is Social Media Important?

Pages and pages (and pages!) of rhetoric has been written about the importance of social media. However, a more applicable question for our purpose here is:

"Why is social media important to YOU, the small business owner, and how do you BEST use it?"

As a small business owner, you are probably used to going to your local Chamber of Commerce or networking event where you pass out your business card and give a 30-60 second commercial about yourself. You understand that these networking events are all based on the premise that you get to know your fellow networkers, and, as you become familiar with each other's products and services you both look for ways to complement each other through professional resources and contacts.

If you have done *a lot* of networking then you probably understand that people will buy *from* (and refer business *to*) people they like. Social media/networking works in much the same way. **When you can successfully create an online profile that is engaging and that people want (and like) to listen to, then you will be able to grow your business offline**.

Outbound vs Inbound Marketing

Traditional marketing consists of *outbound* marketing. These are things like print media, radio and TV, direct mail, cold calls and e-mail blasts. Methods such as these may have worked in the past, but not today. Technological advances like TIVO/DVR, e-mail spam blockers, and caller ID allow consumers to block messages they don't want.

Consumers still, however, DO want to learn about the best products and services for their needs. The key is that they want to find this information *on their own* – most often by using the Internet. And this is where *inbound* marketing comes in. *You get the consumer to come to you* by creating marketing campaigns that pull people into your business. This strategy is called *inbound* marketing.

Inbound marketers offer the public useful information, tools and resources to **attract people to their websites**, while also interacting and developing relationships with consumers on the web. Inbound marketing tools include blogging, content publishing, social media and social networks.

Some Crazy Social Media Statistics

Facebook

- The average Facebook user has 130 friends.
- More than 25 billion pieces of content (i.e. web links, news stories, blog posts, notes, photo albums, etc.) is shared each month.
- Over 300,000 users helped translate the site through the translations application.
- More than 150 million people engage with Facebook on external websites every month.
- Two-thirds of comScore's U.S. Top 100 websites and half of comScore's Global Top 100 websites have integrated with Facebook.
- There are more than 100 million active users currently accessing Facebook through their mobile devices.
- People that access Facebook via mobile are twice as active as non-mobile users (think about that when designing your Facebook page).
- The average Facebook user is connected to 60 pages, groups and events.
- People spend over 500 billion minutes per month on Facebook.

- There are more than 1 million entrepreneurs and developers from 180 countries on Facebook.

Twitter

- Twitter's web platform only accounts for a quarter of its users – 75% use third-party apps.
- Twitter gets more than 300,000 new users every day.
- There are currently 110 million users of Twitter's services.
- Twitter receives 180 million unique visits each month.
- There are more than 600 million searches on Twitter every day.
- Twitter started as a simple SMS-text service.
- Over 60% of Twitter use is outside the U.S.
- There are more than 50,000 third-party apps for Twitter.
- Twitter has donated access to all of its Tweets to the Library of Congress for research and preservation.
- More than one-third of users access Twitter via their mobile phone.

LinkedIn

- LinkedIn is the oldest of the four sites we are discussing, having been created on May 5, 2003.
- There are more than 70 million users worldwide.
- Members of LinkedIn come from more than 200 countries from every continent.

- LinkedIn is available in six native languages – English, French, German, Italian, Portuguese, and Spanish.
- Oracle's Chief Financial Officer, Jeff Epstein, was headhunted for the position via his LinkedIn profile.
- 80% of companies use LinkedIn as a recruitment tool.
- A new member joins LinkedIn every second.
- LinkedIn receives almost 12 million unique visitors per day.

YouTube

- The very first video uploaded was called "Me at the Zoo" on April 23, 2005.
- By June 2006, more than 65,000 videos were being uploaded every day.
- YouTube receives more than 2 billion viewers per day.
- Every minute, 24 hours of video is uploaded to YouTube.
- The U.S. accounts for 70% of YouTube users.
- Over half of YouTube's users are under 20 years old.
- You would need to live for around 1,000 years to watch all the videos currently on YouTube.
- YouTube is available in 19 countries and 12 languages.
- Music videos account for 20% of uploads.

- YouTube uses the same amount of bandwidth as the entire Internet used in 2000.

-

Blogging

- 77% of Internet users read blogs.
- There are currently 133 million blogs listed on leading blog directory, Technorati.
- 60% of bloggers are between the ages of 18-44.
- One in five bloggers update their blogs daily.
- Two thirds of bloggers are male.
- Corporate blogging accounts for 14% of blogs.
- 15% of bloggers spend 10 hours a week blogging.
- More than half of all bloggers are married and/or parents.
- More than 50% of bloggers have more than one blog.

Big Brands Who Do It Well

Best Buy

Best Buy used Twitter to create a "Twelpforce" – an online, Twitter-enabled help force. Consumers can send a Tweet about any consumer electronics or customer service problem to @twelpforce and get an answer from one of the 2,500 employees who share this account.

> **Small Business Application:** *Think about ways you can use Twitter to ask and answer questions.*

Amazon

Amazon's ratings and reviews are among the most sophisticated, with features including reader responses to reviews posted by others, verified reviewer identities, and the ability to see all reviews posted by a reviewer. The recommendations on the site represent a social feature that works without requiring any additional activity from consumers. In addition, Amazon's Kindle includes social features. While reading, you can see what passages other readers have highlighted.

Small Business Application: *Think about ways you can take advantage of ratings and recommendations.*

Zappos

While this online shoe and apparel retailer is now owned by Amazon, it operates separately and includes its own social features. Zappos encourages all of its employees to Tweet (and many of them to blog). This allows the employees to share the customer service interactions they undertake to provide Zappos' legendary service. Zappos' site is filled with Twitter and Facebook "Like" buttons so users can share their opinions of selected items

Small Business Application: *Think about ways you can get your employees involved in your social media efforts.*

Starbucks

Starbucks solicits customer ideas on MyStarbucksIdea.com, an active discussion site with almost 100,000 suggestions on it. And if you've used location-based service, FourSquare, to check-in so frequently at a Starbucks that you've become the "mayor" of that location, you can get product discounts.

Small Business Application: Think about ways to solicit ideas and suggestions from your customers. Bonus Idea – determine what special promotions that you can offer to people who "check-in."

Developing Your Strategy

Marketing Strategy has been a popular buzz phrase in the business community for decades. Now, a new-fangled technology comes along and you, the small business owner, must *also* figure out a *Social Media Strategy*!? It sounds overwhelming, doesn't it? Well, it doesn't have to be.

Let's take a step back and look at the definition of *strategy*:

The word *strategy* comes from the Greek and roughly translated means "to lead into war." YOU are the leader, and your *customers* and *prospects* are your army. Your goal is to lead them into a battle against your competition.

Regardless of the type of project, *strategy* must specify three things: The What, The Where, and The How.

#1 – The What: When you look at *WHAT*, you must think about specific goals and objectives. For example, are there specific products and services that you want to highlight?

#2 – The Where: When deciding a social media strategy, think about the *WHERE* as the *different types* of social media outlets.

#3 – The How: The *HOW,* of course, will be how you decide *to use* social media. Not every social media tool is right for every business.

Let's repeat that together out loud...

"Not <u>every</u> social media tool is right for <u>every</u> business."

Some social media tools, like Facebook, are easier to adapt to most businesses. Others, like YouTube, might not be as applicable. Sure, you might find a small use for it, but your social media campaign does not need to revolve around it.

You should already have a generic marketing plan. If you do NOT have one, then two key marketing factors to start with are *your target market* and your *competition*

Who is Your Target Market?

When you decide to rent a movie, you typically do not base your rental choice on "anything on DVD." You usually have a specific movie (or at least genre) in mind.

You need to do the same thing with defining your target market... if you sell shoes, then your target market should NOT be "anybody with feet."

Take this time to brainstorm and define your target market.

What kinds of things (topics) do you think this market finds interesting? *Name at least 5.*

In your regular marketing plan you should have decided *where* you find your target market. To apply this to social media, think about what social media tools they might use. Are they on Facebook? Twitter? LinkedIn? Do they use FourSquare? Do they *write* blogs? Do they *read* blogs? **Do not hesitate to ask them – and, yes, ask them in-person! Not every component of your social media plan takes place online.** *Use the space below to make some notes.*

Identify Your Competition

There are two different types of competition: Direct Competition and Indirect Competition. If you are a candlestick maker, then direct competitors would be other candlestick makers. However, indirect competitors are makers of items that compete with candlesticks, like lamps and flashlights.

Identify 3 Direct Competitors:

1. _____

2. _____

3. _____

Identify 3 Indirect Competitors:

1. _____

2. _____

3. _____

In a traditional marketing plan, you examine what your competitors are doing well and what they are doing poorly. You also examine what your business is doing well and what your business is doing poorly. This examination helps you determine your opportunities for and threats against your business growth.

Now think about this as it applies to social media and social networks...

Build a chart below to list your direct and indirect competitors. Check off the social networks in which your competition participates.

Now research and think about your competitors. Do you notice anything? What are 3 things that you noticed about 4 of your competitors? Use the space on the next page to write down your notes. Did you notice anything interesting about their Facebook pages? What kinds of things did they post? (Check their walls.) Did they have any special tabs, contests or interesting discussions? Do they have a Twitter account? What kinds of things are they Tweeting about? How many followers do they have? Are they Tweeting anything that could bring them business? What about recommendations on LinkedIn? Do they have any videos on YouTube?

Developing Your "Pitch"

We have argued the importance of a proper Unique Selling Pitch (USP) many times in the past. Today, however, it is even *more* important to establish (and promote) your USP. Why? **Because your goal is to break through all of the of online and social media clutter** that your target market has to sort through each and every day.

Most business owners do not have a USP – most have a "me too" pitch which feeds solely upon the sheer momentum of the marketplace. They promise no great value, benefit, or service – just a "buy from us" for no justifiable or rational reason.

Positioning is about making your offering different from – and more valuable than – your competitors' offerings. You then consistently follow that up with the placement of that idea in the minds of your target group of customers.

A well-developed pitch/positioning attracts customers by creating a positive and unique identity for your company and its offerings. Positioning is vital for distinguishing your offering from everybody else's. In short, **your positioning affects every aspect of your communications – and your business.** Or, at least it *should*.

It's absolutely KEY to put yourself in your customers' shoes. Look at your product or service from the point of view of someone thinking about buying it. What would be a compelling reason for that customer to buy from *you* instead of *your competition*?

What is Your Goal?

For an effective social media strategy, you need to have a clear purpose in mind. Have you decided what your focus will be? Do you want brand awareness? How about customer loyalty? Or is your focus just on sales? Each plays a key role in your business. Remember that you need to enter into your strategy with clear purpose. If you do not have a clear *purpose*; you will not receive a clear *result*.

It is okay to change this focus later. In fact, it's natural for your focus to change over time as your business grows and your campaigns change.

For the majority of companies that utilize social media, brand awareness is the reason for their campaign. Brand awareness is about spreading a message, so the more content the better.

What if your strategy is to build customer loyalty? This should be an overall perspective of your social media strategy. You want to engage with people in such a way that makes them interested in what you are posting. And how do you "make" customers loyal? Value is the key. Provide value to them, make your solution the *best* solution. Then they won't even *consider* looking elsewhere.

> **If your strategy is to build brand awareness, then <u>what is your brand message (i.e. your USP)</u>?** (Hint: We just discussed this in the last section.)

Obviously sales are important for businesses. However, social media marketing is much more than just sales. Social media is about connecting a problem (something your customer has) with a solution (something you offer) by creating a friend (or relationship) first. Sure, you can ask for the sale up-front, but expect a low conversion rate if you do. Ask for a relationship and you'll have a better chance of brand loyalty (i.e. repeat sales).

Humans Build the Best Relationships

Building social media relationships works best when you "remain human". But what does that mean? And how do you accomplish this?

Do NOT Advertise by Shouting. Social media is NOT about you – **it's about the image you project**. It's about being transparent and giving your target market a reason to interact with you. If you're consistently asking for sales and promoting discounts then chances are your target market will start ignoring you.

Commit...and Don't Rush the Process. Social media is not a *'right now, today'* business tool. To reiterate...**it does NOT provide you with instant results.** Social media takes months of hard work to establish a reputation and build your social network...even longer to generate a solid ROI for your efforts.

Remember to Contribute. If you want to establish a good relationship with someone, you have to **GIVE them something before asking for something in return**. Social media requires you to contribute to the community in a meaningful or useful way on a regular basis before you attempt to get something in return. Contributions don't have to be big. Things like sharing interesting or useful links or offering free help and advice (with no expectation of reward or recognition of course) are great places to start.

Stay the Same. If you're going to create a brand for yourself on social media, then **your brand needs to remain constant**. Make sure that your Twitter name, your Facebook page and everything else about you on social media networks make it clear *who you are* and *who your company is*. It's important that customers be able to easily recognize your brand when they go to each of these sites so that your name sticks out in their minds.

Facebook

Getting Started: Why Do I Want to Be on Facebook?

Facebook is a social utility for connecting people with those around them – friends, family, coworkers, or simply others with similar interests. Facebook started in 2004 as a closed community for college students (requiring users to sign up with a valid university e-mail address) but has since expanded beyond that to high schools, corporations, regional networks, or any user across the world. Facebook allows users to connect and share information in a variety of ways.

> **Tip!** Make sure that your Twitter name, your Facebook page and everything else about you on social media networks make it clear *who you are* and *who your company is* and *what your company represents.*

Meet your peers. Facebook is not just for college kids anymore. One of the fastest growing segments on Facebook are those over the age of 35.

Build relationships. By engaging in conversations with your prospects and customers, you can better adapt your marketing and business services to meet their needs. Think of it as a 24/7 market research tool.

Raise visibility. By consistently showing up, posting relevant information, and being a thought leader, you can increase visibility and credibility as an expert (even THE expert) in your area.

Develop your personal brand. The lines between business and personal have become blurred. You can reveal as much or as little about yourself as you wish, allowing you to personalize your brand.

> **Think about it!** If you are interested in marketing to your target market and other audiences, you should understand the medium.

Facebook Basics: Joining Facebook

On Facebook, *profiles* are meant for *people* and *pages* are meant for *businesses*. To fully engage and leverage Facebook's features, you should create a personal profile.

What NOT to do with your personal profile? Do NOT create a personal profile for your business.

> ### Business Pages vs. Personal Profiles
>
> Pages allow you to designate multiple administrators so that you can have multiple people help manage the account. This is nice because if one of your administrators leaves the company, you can still have control over the page.
>
> Pages are, by default, public and will start ranking in Facebook and public search results.
>
> Pages are split into different categories (i.e. local businesses, brands, musicians, etc.) that help you get listed in more relevant search results.
>
> *Personal profiles* have *friends* (which require mutual acceptance), but *anyone* can become a fan of your page without first going through administrator approval.

Remember...*profiles* are for *people*. *Pages* are for *businesses*.

Facebook is building significant new functionality for businesses, and all of this functionality is only available to pages (not profiles). We'll talk about pages more in a later section.

Facebook Profile

Tour of a User Profile

News Feed

Found in the center column of your home page, the news feed is the constantly updating list of stories from profiles and pages that you follow on Facebook.

In addition to posts from friends and pages you follow, you'll see photo tags, friend requests, event RSVPs and group memberships in the news feed. The news feed algorithm bases the information that appears there on various factors (i.e. how many friends are commenting on a certain piece of content, who posted the content, and what type of content it is, such as photos, videos, or status updates).

The "Like" Button

Clicking on "Like" is a way to give positive feedback or to connect with things you care about on Facebook. You can like content that your friends post to give them feedback or you can like a page that you want to connect with and follow on Facebook. You can also connect to content. When you click "Like" on a Page, in an advertisement, or on content off of Facebook, you are making a connection.

This connection will be displayed in your profile and on your wall and your friends may receive a news feed story about the connection. You may be displayed on the page you connected to, in advertisements about that page, or in social plug-ins next to the content you like. Once you "like a page," the page may also post content into your news feed or send you messages. You may also share this connection with applications on the Facebook platform.

You always have control over your connections. You can "unlike" most content immediately, manage your connections on your profile, and restrict who you share your connections with in your privacy settings.

Fan Pages vs. Groups

Facebook Pages

Facebook offers you Facebook *pages*. What does that mean? You can use Facebook pages to create and give your business its own profile on Facebook. And right now, these pages are free. A page gives your business an identity on Facebook which then strengthens your brand. Current customers or even potential customers can become *fans* of your page. By becoming your fan, this allows them to follow you and receive any updates that you post to your page.

The great thing about Facebook pages is that every time someone becomes a fan of your page all of *their* friends see that they have become one of your fans. This often attracts other followers AND creates a buzz regarding your business and, of course, your Facebook page.

You can use your Facebook page to not only share your company information, but you can also use it to post photos, videos, applications, and messages. Any activity that you perform on your Facebook business page is then broadcasted into the news feed column of your followers.

When creating your Facebook page, there are things to keep in mind. You'll be asked whether your page is about a local business, a brand /product, or an artist/band/public figure.

Each of these categories will provide you with an opportunity to complete your "basic information," "detailed information," or your "contact information." Each option will provide you with a page that enables you to provide different ways of showing your information.

Don't Stress; Facebook now allows you to change your category and page name as long as you have less than 100 Likes. It is also important to remember that the page type you select will categorize your page with other similar pages in that category.

Facebook Groups

There is a BIG difference between a *fan page* and a *group*. They can both be useful, but they have drastically different functions. To create either, you must have a personal profile on Facebook. You don't want to create a profile for your business or you will be in violation of Facebook's Terms of Service and will risk having that profile deleted.

Both *pages* and *groups* can give your business an identity on Facebook which then strengthens your brand. Current customers or even potential customers can become fans of your page or join your group. The awesome thing about this is that every time someone becomes a fan of your page or joins your group all of *their* friends see that they have become your *fan* or *member*. This often attracts other followers AND creates a buzz for your page or group.

We assist in the administration of both *fan pages* and *groups*. And honestly, for the purposes of business and branding, we prefer building fan pages. We do not recommend that a small business start a "group." See why on the next page...

The Big Differences: Fan Page vs. Group

Status Updates

A *fan page* looks just like a *profile page*, except that it is for your *business*. A fan page, just like your personal profile, allows you to update its status. The status updates will appear on news feeds of all of its fans the same way your personal status updates appears on news feeds of all your friends.

A Facebook group cannot update its status. Individuals can write on a group's wall, but the group's wall posts will NOT show up in your news feed or in the feeds belonging to the group's members.

Corporate Identity

Facebook considers a group to be an extension of your personal actions. When you post something as a group administrator, it appears to be coming from you and is attached to your personal profile. Alternately, pages can create content that comes from the page itself. That content doesn't have to be linked to you personally.

Applications

Facebook allows you to add applications to your fan page but NOT to your group. You can add an application to your business page that is customized with your own corporate identity or branding.

Search Visibility

Another advantage of a fan page is that they are searchable by Google. Also, another related key difference is that pages are indexed by external search engines, such as Google, just like public profile pages. Groups are not.

Creating a Fan Page

Facebook Pages are the best way for businesses and organizations to interact with consumers and the public at large. Facebook Pages allow consumers to "like" them, which is displayed to the user's feed. It allows you to provide information about your business or organization all in one place.

Unlike a regular Facebook account, there is no limit to the number of followers or likes you can get.

Here's how to setup a Facebook page, along with a few tips on creating a great profile.

Step 1: Create a Page

On your left hand sidebar, locate the subheading called "Pages." Hover your mouse there. A button called "more" will appear. Click that button.

On the next page, click "Create a Page" in the upper right corner.

(Or Go to http://www.facebook.com/pages/create.php)

Step 2: Select what type of page you want.

Each page has slightly different options. For example, with a local business you can provide information like hours and parking options. With a cause,

you can provide options like donations.

Create a name for your page. Pick either your business name or something that describes your business.

Tip! If you select "Local Business or Place," you must enter an address. This will allow your fans to "check-in" to your business. Checking-in is something that Facebook users can do from their mobile devices. Think about how you can incorporate the number of "Check-Ins" with a special promotion.

Click "Get Started"

Enter the information for your business. This is the bare minimum of information that Facebook needs to get you started.

Choose your category carefully, as it can help people find you in the future. If in doubt, visit some of your competitors' Pages and see what categories they're using

Step 3: Upload a Picture

Your profile image makes a *huge* difference on people's overall impression of your page and your brand.

Choose an image that represents what you stand for and would be instantly recognizable. If there are multiple Pages with the same name, people will use your image to make sure they're choosing the right page.

Step 4: Enter Your Basic Information:

Fill out the information as thoroughly as possible, but do not stress over it. You can come back to this at any time. Keep in mind that Google (and other search engines) can crawl (or read) this information. So it is wise to use terms and keywords that you want the search engines to link to your business.

Step 5: Create your Custom URL

In the old days you had to wait until you had atleast 25 fans.

But now Facebook is allowing people to create their own URL during the set up. Pick something as short as possible because you can use it later to attract fans & likes.

You can tell your Fans to text "Like <*your username*> 32665" to become fans, so if you choose something really long, like BobsSuperAwesomeHotdogFanpage it will make this fan attraction tactic a little tricky.

Customizing Your Fan Page

Add a Cover Photo

Just like with your personal profile, Facebook now also allows you to upload a cover photo to your Facebook Page. This is a great way to show what your business is all about, but according to Facebook's terms, it is not meant to be space for an advertisement. Nor are you allowed to upload images that are primarily text. Use this space to showcase a great visual that makes your business stand out.

When you view your page, you'll see an option to either add a cover photo or to change your cover photo, if you've added one previously.

 You can then upload a photo from your computer or choose one from photos you've already added to your Facebook Page. The end result looks something like this and will appear across your Facebook Page. It's a very big visual, so use it to your advantage.

The first and most important step in creating your Facebook Timeline business page is creating your Facebook Timeline cover art. Keep in mind that search engines are responsible for

7% of the traffic referred to Facebook. So for many people, your Facebook page may be their first introduction to your business.

Cover Art Design Considerations

If you had a Facebook page for your business before the timeline changes then you might be a little confused at first as landing pages no longer exist on the platform. Instead your Facebook Timeline business page now functions as your landing page. So invest some thought and time into designing cover art that visually represents your brand.

Consider all of the important elements of design including:

- Font style and size
- Color combinations
- Images and symbols

Be creative when designing your cover art. Choose the colors, images and font that will best represent your brand. Keep in mind that your profile image will be your business logo and will appear as a small square in the lower left corner of your cover art. Because of this, the design elements of your cover art should complement your logo.

You might also consider adding a few words to your cover art that sum up your business. Something memorable like:

- Reach out and Touch Someone (AT&T)
- It's Everywhere You Want to Be (VISA)
- The Quicker Picker-Upper (Bounty)

If you don't have time to create the cover art yourself, or if you aren't especially creative, or you simply feel overwhelmed at the whole process, you can always outsource the design work.

Facebook Cover Art Rules

Regardless of whether you create the cover art yourself or you hire someone else to do it, make sure you know what Facebook requires. For example, (At the time of this writing) the cover art needs to be 851X315 pixels. In addition, the design must comply with the Facebook cover art rules.

Facebook cover art may not include:

- Pricing information
- Contact information – no email, phone, etc...
- References to Facebook features – like, share, etc...
- A call to action

Be sure to read all the details on the Facebook Cover Art Rules before designing your cover.

Uploading Your Facebook Cover Art

Once you've settled on a design, go to your Facebook Timeline business page to upload it. Remember, you manage your business page through your personal profile so the first step is to login to Facebook.

Then, in the upper right hand corner you will see a drop-down arrow. Click the arrow and then click on the business page you created the cover art for. Once you're on your business page click the "add a cover" button to upload the design.

Create Facebook Fanpage Tabs/Apps

Apps add functionality and interactivity to Facebook Timeline – something your followers, clients and customers are most likely addicted to, if they are at all representative of mobile and social media users today.

An example: You can "nudge" them into boosting your local business presence by using Facebook apps like FourSquare yourself (when they click on the app link, they quickly find out how to install FourSquare for themselves). You can boost your Timeline results by adding commands such as "Like us with FourSquare" on your website or blog.

There are literally hundreds of Timeline apps available for you to install and post about to your readers and followers (with more being added daily). Suit the app to your target customer demographic – for example, if you are targeting the eighteen to thirty-four-year-old age groups, you might want to share favorite songs through Spotify.

Tip! If your target demographic is mostly female and seems to enjoy sharing images, you really do need to install the Pinterest app. Sign up on Pinterest and start creating Pinboard yourself! (And be sure to install the "Pinit" sharing icon on all your website photos).

In the old days, before Timeline you used to be able to build a "default landing tab" – a page inside of your Fanpage that nonfans would land on by default (while current fans would default to your wall).

With the new timeline layout Facebook provides four spaces for app icons. The first space, immediately to the right of the about section, will always (until Facebook changes it!) be your "Photos" app. It will always display the most recent picture you uploaded to your wall. Currently it cannot be moved, modified, or altered. The other three spaces are flexible and offer a lot of opportunity for moving your business forward.

Organizing Your Facebook Timeline Apps

With the timeline update you can no longer set a "default" tab, but that does not mean that a custom page or "app" is not useful. Some social media marketing experts think that "in order to succeed in Facebook, companies need access to the advanced capabilities that apps provide." These apps help companies customize their Fan Pages, to add custom "Tabs" (or pages) and to add advanced capabilities via specialized apps such as video players, contests, fan-only content, email opt-in forms, or integrations with other social media platforms like Pinterest and Twitter.

You can have a maximum of 14 apps in your Facebook Timeline; however at there are just four spaces for apps at the top of the Timeline near the lower edge of your cover art design. Facebook has predetermined the first app, but you can choose the other three.

Some ideas for apps for those three slots include:

- Likes - showing the number of people who have liked your page (Shown by default, but unless your likes are impressive, I would use a different
- Twitter
- YouTube
- Pinterest
- Map of the physical location of your business
- Upcoming events
- Merchandise

Keep in mind that these three apps can be changed, switched around or modified. You can even modify the image and name of third-party apps here as well. And, best of all, this is where you can include a call to action!

It's important to note that apps need to be 111X74 pixels.

Changes to Apps

Once you've added your apps you may leave them there forever – or at least until Facebook implements another design update. On the other hand, you may decide to swap one or more of your current apps out with apps that aren't currently visible to those visiting your Facebook Timeline business page.

Let's say for example that because your page is so new you have very few "likes." So you instead chose to display the Twitter, Pinterest and YouTube apps. Once you've received the number of "likes" you feel comfortable displaying publically you might want to swap out one of the social media apps for the "like" app.

To switch apps around you:

- Click the small triangle to the right of the fourth app

- Hover over the app you want to change out

- You will see a small pencil icon appear in the upper right corner of the app

- Click on the pencil icon

- Click on the name of the app you want to in that space – in this case the "like" app

The "like" app will then replace the app you were hovering over so that visitors to your page will now be able to see the number of likes your page has received. This is important because a high number of "likes" offers the "social proof" that is becoming increasingly important for credibility.

Favorite Landing Page Developer (3rd Party Apps)

In the "old days" one was able to create a custom landing tab using a Facebook app called "Custom FBML". At that time you could copy and paste code (HTML) into the application and it would display. This was a gold mine for savvy web developers that wanted to dive into the social media marketing world. Since the timeline update "Custom FBML" is no longer available and the easiest way to install a custom tab is to subscribe to a 3rd party Custom Tab Developer. ...And there are a ton of them out there; of course my two favorites are Lujure and ShortStackApps

Lujure has a free plan and a plan that starts around $30. Lujure is probably the most simple and easy to use Custom Page Developer out there. The have features that allow you to drag and drop special applications- like a shopping cart or a mobile version of your website into your Facebook page. Go fan then on their Facebook page and check out one of their webinars. Unlike some of the other Fanpage software vendors Lujure lets you install your custom apps to as many pages as you want regardless of how many fans you have..http://www. Facebook.com/Lujure

ShortStackApps is a little more consuming. It works best for people who have a basic understanding of HTML and CSS. So if you are a person who likes to custom code your Constant Contact emails then ShortStack is for you. You will want to know how to create your own custom graphics. This is an affordable option for people who want to white label the creation several Facebook Tabs in multiple pages.

Create Other Page Administrators (Admins)

Why? Because, if for some crazy reason your profile page is deleted, then all of your pages will be deleted as well. Also, it is nice to have help creating your Facebook page. Remember, social media is about *community* content.

How to Add Other Admins

You should see a section labeled "Admins." Click "Add." From here you can select friends (off your friends list or you can type in the name of the person you would like to promote to Admin). You also can add an Admin via e-mail.

Assign Roles to Fan page Administrators

Along with some of the Timeline changes, Facebook now makes it easy for Page owners to specify specific roles to page admins.

Manager: can manage admin roles, send messages and create posts as the Page, create ads, and view insights. **Managers are the only administrators that can manage the page settings** – such as publishing/unpublishing or deleting the page.

Content Creator: can edit the Page, send messages and create posts as the Page, create ads, and view insights.

Moderator: Can respond to and delete comments on the Page, send messages as the Page, create ads, and view insights.

Advertiser: Can create ads and view insights.

Insight Analyst: Can view insights.

Creating Engaging Content

Creating engaging content is probably the most important and one of the most potentially difficult components of having a successful Facebook campaign. You will see that a lot of social marketing companies tout that the number #1 Facebook error is not having a landing tab. Some of these companies sell tab design services, others sell the html code/script, and other sell – well, who knows what? You could have a fan page that attracts 15,000 "likes" in the first month that it is published, but if you're not getting feedback and fan engagement then you're wasting your time. And, technically, it's not that difficult to create engaging content. It just takes a little bit of time, planning, and commitment. Find three businesses that interest you and then "like" them (a.k.a. "become a fan").

They don't have to be in your field, but you do have to be interested in what they have to say. Go to their profile and look at their "wall." (After you have "liked" them you should be able to click their profile picture and be taken to their wall.)

Here are some ideas of things you can post to your fan page.

- **Links to YOUR eNewsletter**. As soon as you publish your newsletter, post the link so that all of your friends and fans can read it or subscribe to it if they're not already on your mailing list.

- **Links to Other Relevant eNewsletters**. Do you subscribe to any newsletters that might be interesting to your audience? We're obsessed with Dr. Mercola's newsletters and articles. Frequently, I post links to his stories on my personal page. However, since he is in the nutrition/natural health market, I will post these links to my clients that are in the same field (a chiropractor, for example).

- **Links to Articles**. Create Google Alerts for topics that your audience would find interesting.

- **Polls/Questions**. What is your favorite Thanksgiving tradition? Do you have any holiday traditions that are unique to YOUR family?

Create Photo Albums

Create photo albums that are relevant to your business. Post pictures of yourself and your employees doing things that are related to your company. Show off a portfolio or take pictures at networking and Chamber events. Take advantage of the mobile upload option...if you have a smartphone -- use it!

Ask your fans to upload pictures! Don't be afraid to let your favorite clients become brand ambassadors.

Import Blogs

There are many ways that you can import a blog. It all depends on how you want to integrate.

There are a number of applications written by various developers. The best bet is to browse through Facebook's Application Directory at:

http://www.facebook.com/apps/

NetworkedBlogs is one of the most popular. It allows you to import your blog both into your personal profile and business page. It also lets you list your blog so that others who are searching for content to read can find your writings.

Create a Schedule

Don't be afraid to get creative and test new waters. Ask your followers what type of contests they want to see. Successful marketing is all about trying new and UNIQUE ways to present your message to your target audience.

Brainstorm: What can you do on a weekly basis?

Tip! Schedule this in your Outlook as a weekly reminder. Posting to ALL social networks shouldn't take much more than 15 minutes.

Once-a-Week Posts. Ritz Pix offers a "Facebook Friday" special every Friday where they offer 50% off their photo books. Think about a special product or service that you might be able to offer. Or, Got Print routinely has a "Trivia Tuesday"... they find random trivia and post it every Tuesday.

Other Ideas:

- Post an Ole and Lena joke every Wednesday. (We're from Minnesota where Ole and Lena jokes thrive!)

- Post favorite recipes, or ask for recipes.

- Post pictures of events/projects.

- Ask for pictures of _____ (fill in the blank with a different subject every week). If there was a new snowfall, ask for snow pictures. If it's spring, ask for your fans' favorite spring flower picture. (Hint: Reward participation. Randomly give something to people who are active and participate on your page.)

If you post a trivia question and only have one response, post that that person wins a $5 Starbucks Gift Card. However, due to Facebook's Terms and Conditions, don't say that you're having a "contest." All contests on Facebook pages must be handled through a 3rd party application.

Daily Posts. Write questions, comments, anecdotes – anything that you think will be interesting to your audience. Be personal. Almost anything that you post on your personal page can apply to your business page. Okay...so you might not want to post a funny story about your daughter spitting up all over your new blouse, but if you noticed a funny commercial or sign, feel free to comment on that. Since we work in marketing, we frequently comment about funny commercials. Below are some other ideas of things you can post to your fan page.

Make Sure You Vary Your Posts. Do not ALWAYS post links to the same website. If you do, people will start to tune you out. Make it varied and interesting. Remember that all you're doing is having a conversation with people. The SAME conversation that you'd have with them in real life, except that you're online. Remember that you're limited to using 140 characters. (Well, you can use more than 140 on Facebook. But if you want to link it to Twitter, I recommend that you stick as close to 140 characters as possible.)

Think about 10 topics that are relevant to your business. Write them down.

Promoting Your Fan Page

If you're going to spend the time (and potentially, the money) to work on using a Facebook page, then don't forget to promote it.

Take advantage of as many opportunities to plug your Facebook page as possible. Put links to it on...

- Your website
- In your e-mail signature
- On your blog
- On your business card
- On every piece of marketing collateral printed

The #1 goal is that you TELL PEOPLE! Your clients need to know that you're using Facebook as an outreach tool.

The "Like Box"

The "like box" is a Facebook widget that enables Facebook page owners to attract and gain likes from their own websites. The like box enables users to see how many users already like this page (and which of their users' friends like it, too), read recent posts from the page, and like the page with one click…all without needing to visit the actual page itself.

You can build your like box by:

- Clicking "Edit Page"
- Then "Marketing"
- Then "Build a Like Box for your Website"

Simply customize it any way you want and then click on "get code" and copy/paste it into your website.

(Or have your Web Maven to do it for you!)

TWITTER

Twitter is an information network. Millions of people, organizations, and businesses use it to discover and share new information. On Twitter, anyone can read, write, and share messages of up to 140 characters. These messages (called Tweets) are public and available to anyone interested in them.

Twitter users subscribe to your messages by following your account. Followers receive every one of your messages in their timeline, a feed of all the accounts they have subscribed to. From a computer or from a phone, Twitter users can elect to receive text message updates when your account Tweets.

Mobile notifications can be a great way to promote exclusive content or coupons, as well as other promotions. If someone has signed up to be notified of your Tweets, then whenever you Tweet they'll get it as an SMS message on their phone. When you combine messages that are quick to write, easy to read, public, opt-in, and accessible anywhere, you have a powerful, real-time way of communicating.

Getting Started on Twitter

First things first – create an account. However, before signing up decide whether you want a *personal* or a *business* Twitter account (or both). Both types of accounts are good for a company to have, but they each serve different purposes.

Company account. A company account represents the company as a whole. Use this type of account to:

- Keep your customer base up-to-date on your events
- Promote recent blog articles or news
- Update your consumers about products/services
- Give real-time updates at conferences and events

Personal account. A personal account is used by an individual employee at the company. This account type is more personalized. It can be used to talk about non-company related things and is better for direct relationship-building. Use this type of account to:

- Act as a liaison to the public for your company
- Update people on what you're working on
- Share tidbits about your personality
- Expand your company's network and make connections

I have both: @MktplaceMaven (Business) and @SocialMediaRach (personal). There is nothing wrong with using both, but I would recommend with starting out with only one or the other.

Decide on a Twitter Name

Your username (a.k.a."handle") is very important. This name will be how people will refer to you on Twitter, and potentially how people will acknowledge you if you ever meet any of your Twitter followers offline.

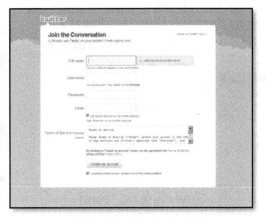

Think of your Twitter handle as your personal brand name. That's how important it is.

Ideas for Twitter Handles:

- Your full name
- A variation of your name (BSmith)
- A combination of your name and your company (CandlestickBob)
- A combination of your name and your industry (CndleJane)
-

After you choose your handle and click "Create my account". Congratulations – you are now a Tweeter!

Twitter Handle DON'TS:

Don't make your Twitter handle something completely random (TigerMan). This is a lost branding opportunity for you and your company.

Find a Few People to Follow

After the account set-up process, Twitter will prompt you to select 10 (or so) interests. Just browse through the topic and pick a few things that interest you. Perhaps there is a local art museum, local anchorman, national retail store or restaurant

(some of these companies Tweet specials and if you mention the specials at their location you get something free).

Now click on "Find Friends." Twitter will bring you to a screen asking you to check if your e-mail contacts are already on Twitter. If you have a Gmail, Hotmail or Yahoo account, feel free to see if anyone you know is already signed up. If you do decide to check, beware of the prompt asking if you'd like to invite them all to Twitter. This will send a message to all your contacts. (Of course, this is NOT a required step. Feel free to skip if you want.)

Personalize Your Profile

The easiest way to personalize your profile is to follow the

---

built-in prompts that Twitter offers.

Just click on "Upload a profile picture" or "Write a short bio." Remember that it is important to personalize your account *before* you begin interacting and following people. If you start following people without a personalized profile, it is less likely that person will follow you back. You may even be mistaken for a spammer.

Your profile is where you can reference your company, your

website, talk about your interests, and list your location. If you are setting up a personal account, I recommend that you use your REAL name. If you are setting up a business account then list your business name. Do not forget to add a picture of you (also called your avatar). It's important to put a face to your name. Pick a nice, smiley photo to represent you. (If you're creating a company account, use your logo.)

If you're concerned about privacy, click the "Account" button.

The last option in profile settings is the "Protect my updates" box. By clicking this, your Twitter stream will be private, and no one will be able to see your updates without following you.

If you want to use Twitter to attract new customers and followers, then it is NOT recommend that you click this option. Many people judge whether to follow someone back through the type of information they Tweet. You are as valuable as your updates, so don't keep people from getting a peek!

If you're worried about random people or strangers seeing your updates, remember that you're in complete control over what you say. But feel comfortable being you.

To further personalize the look of

your Twitter profile, go to the Design tab to create a customized theme or background.

Many marketers and social media experts say, "All the best dressed Twitterers have custom backgrounds."

Play with the different colors that represent your company's logo or add a background image that you like! If you're setting up a company Twitter account, it is probably a good idea to use colors and images that match the branding that you use everywhere else. Remember...you want people to recognize you. You want a similar look/feel for ALL your profiles (and website, business cards, and all other sales collateral).

Once you have your profile looking the way you want then click on "Home" (in the menu at the top of the screen).

Start Tweeting

Even before finding people to follow, we recommend Tweeting a few things that will give people an idea of the type of content

you'll be Tweeting. Your most valuable asset is the information you provide.

Types of Tweets:

- **An observation:** Tweet about what you're doing, thinking or feeling
- **What you're reading**: Post a link to an interesting blog post or news article
- **What you're watching:** Post a link to a cool video from Hulu or YouTube
- **What events you're going to:** Share a link to the next conference you plan to attend
- **Promote your content:** Post a link to your most recent company or personal blog article
- **Promote someone else's content:** Post a link to someone else's blog article as a helpful resource
- **Chat with someone:** Send messages using an @ sign (to be explained later)
- **Retweet what someone else has said:** Retweet (using RT or Retweet in the beginning of the message) to repeat what someone else has said

Remember that everything you say online is public!

Don't tweet anything you wouldn't say in public at a networking event. Even if you delete a Tweet, it might still be archived on the Internet and could be found.

Find More People to Follow

Building your network is the most challenging and time-consuming part of using Twitter. Expanding your network doesn't happen immediately. You need to commit and take the time to use Twitter effectively.

By following people, you will receive their updates on a regular basis in your Twitter stream. This is your chance to learn about their lives, check out the blog posts they are reading and meet the people they interact with. Following a good-sized community can be valuable and fun!

Twitter Search: This free resource is a search function that helps you find people who are Tweeting about specific words. For example, you can find people who have Tweeted about "candlesticks." Just

type your search term in the field at the top of the screen and click "Enter." Alternatively, you can go to http://search.twitter.com.

Follow people talking about the topics you enjoy. (Also, use Twitter search to see who has Tweeted about your company.)

Follow People Your Followers are Following: Once you begin receiving updates from a handful of people, watch to see who those people chat with using @reply. Maybe that person would be fun to follow as well!

Follow Thought Leaders or Bloggers: See if any of your favorite bloggers are on Twitter. Many bloggers include a link to their Twitter account in their sidebar or personal info section on their website.

Follow Hashtags (#) at Events: At many events, the organizer will establish a hashtag so anyone Tweeting at the event can include the hashtag (#) in their Tweet. Follow those people who are at the same event as you whom you may not have met in person yet.

Tip! Collect People's Twitter Names at Events

Like we said before, many social media-savvy people will include their Twitter handles on their nametags at an event. Write down their names and follow them later. You can find their Twitter account by adding their handle to the end of http://twitter.com/USERNAME.

For example, if someone tells you to "follow MktplaceMaven" you can type 'http://twitter.com/ MktplaceMaven' in your browser's navigation bar to find us. If you are not sure if someone you just met is on Twitter – ask!

Get People to Follow You

Following people and receiving their updates is great. In order to have valuable two-way conversations, however, you need people to follow you back and receive your updates as well.

This is why it is important to fully set up your profile before reaching out to a large number of people for new connections. If you follow someone who doesn't already know you, you need to have sufficient information about you in your profile so that person can make the decision as to whether or not to follow you back.

> **Don't follow too many people at once:** Best practice is to follow no more than 25-50 people a day because there will be a time gap between following people and having them follow you back. If your profile says you are following 2,000 people and only 30 followers have followed you back so far, it appears that 1970 of those who you followed *chose not to follow you back*. This unfavorable ratio makes you look like a bad person to add to one's network. Wait a little bit to give people the chance to follow you back before finding a new batch of people to add to your network.

Having followers is important because they are the network group who will see your Tweets. (Remember, on Facebook our goal is to gain "friends" or have people "like" your page.) It is much the same way on Twitter. Think of your total number of followers as your Twitter "friends."

Make your company's Twitter usernames easy to find. If more than one person at your company uses Twitter, create a page that lists all the Twitter handles of the people in your company. By giving your customers an easy way to interact with individual people, it helps them get to know the type of people who work at your company. It also gives insight to your brand!

Make your Tweets useful resources so people need you. *You are what you Tweet.* People will want to follow you if they think they will get value from your content. You want to avoid making your Twitter account purely a promotional tool.

Interact with those people you follow who don't follow you back yet. Make sure to monitor your Twitter stream. Comment on what people are saying...give feedback...compliment people. The key is to engage.

Engage With Your Network: Reply and Mention

What is an @Reply? An @reply is any update posted by clicking the "Reply" button on another Tweet. (When you hover over a Tweet, you will see three options: Favorite, Retweet, and Reply.)

People say lots of things on Twitter and sometimes you want to say something back. Your reply will always begin with @username (insert username of the person you are replying to). Anyone Tweet that is a reply to you will show up in your @Mentions tab on your homepage.

To post a reply on Twitter:

Find the Tweet you want to react to on Twitter.

Hover your mouse over their message and click the "reply" icon.

Complete your Tweet in the box that pops up, and click "Tweet" to send it.

In order to send a message to another person on Twitter, you need to use an @ before the person's name. Think of it as the "address" of the Tweet. This type of message is still public and viewable by anyone in the world.

By putting @USERNAME at the beginning of your Tweet, Twitter knows who to send it to. This type of Tweet is also

called a reply or @reply (pronounced "at reply"). All of the @replies you receive will go into your @Mentions tab.

What is an @Mention? An @mention is any Twitter update that contains @username anywhere in the body of the tweet. (Yes, this means that replies are also considered mentions.)

Things to Note:

-People will only see others' replies in their home timeline if they are following both the sender and recipient of the update.

-People will see any mentions posted by someone they follow (all mentions are treated like regular Tweets).

-People with protected accounts can only send replies to people they have approved to follow them.

-If someone sends you a reply and you are not following the user, the reply will not appear on your home timeline. That reply will appear in your mentions timeline.

To see what message they replied to in your timeline, just click any space around the Tweet and your details pane will open to display the Tweet they replied to, as well as other content related to the message.

What's a Message? (Formerly Called a Direct Message)

A message (previously called a direct message) is a private message sent via Twitter to one of your followers. **(This is different than mentions and @replies.)** In turn, people you follow can send you a private message. You cannot send a direct message to a user who is not following you. How to Send a Private Message via the Web:

- Login to your Twitter account.
- Click the "Messages" button on the top menu bar of your page.
- You'll land on a page showing your private messages history. Click the "New Message" button. Click to send a new message.
- In the pop-up box, type the name or username of the person you wish to send to.
- Enter the message you wish and click "Send."

You may only send a direct message to your followers.

Understanding Private Messages:

- Direct messages behave more like Tweets than e-mails. The sender or recipient of a DM can delete the message, and it will disappear from both sender and recipient inboxes.

- The number next to your direct messages tab reflects the number of direct messages in your inbox.

- If this number has changed recently and you have not deleted any of your messages, remember that the sender of the direct message has the ability to delete messages from your inbox. These messages are not mysteriously disappearing or getting lost.

-

What Does Twitter Do For Businesses?

As a business, you can use Twitter to quickly share information, gather market intelligence and insights, and build relationships with people who care about your company. Often, there is already a conversation about your business happening on Twitter. Build your following, reputation, and customer's trust with these simple practices:

- **Share.** Share photos and behind-the-scenes info about your business. Even better, give a glimpse of developing projects and events. Users come to Twitter to get and share the latest, so give it to them!

- **Listen.** Regularly monitor the comments about your company, brand, and products.

- **Ask.** Ask questions of your followers to glean valuable insights and show that you are listening.

- **Respond.** Respond to compliments and feedback in real-time.

- **Reward.** Tweet updates about special offers, discounts and time-sensitive deals.

- **Demonstrate wider leadership and know-how.** Reference articles and links about the bigger picture as it relates to your business. Champion your stakeholders. Retweet and reply publicly to great Tweets posted by your followers and customers.

- **Establish the right voice.** Twitter users tend to prefer a direct, genuine, and likable tone from your business, but think about your voice as you Tweet. How do you want your business to appear to the Twitter community?

Use Twitter for Marketing

Use Twitter to drive people to your company's website. Tweet about interesting resources your employees have posted on your blog or website. Have you recently published a report or newsletter that people can download for free? Tweet about it, linking back to the download page on your website. If the content on your site is truly remarkable, people may start Tweeting about it on their own! They can share your resource to their friends on Twitter.

Tip! Twitter "Favorites" as Testimonials

Underneath each Tweet in your Twitter stream, there is a

little star. When you click the little star, that Tweet gets added to your Favorites tab. As you track what people are saying about your company in Twitter search, add all of the positive Tweets to your Favorites.

The next time someone asks about your company, send them the link to your Favorites page. The URL for this page will be: *http://twitter.com/USERNAME/favorites*

Monitor your brand on Twitter. Using the Twitter search tool (http://search.twitter.com), you can search and track what people are saying about your company, products, competitors or any other hot words in your industry. Set up an RSS feed to receive all search results in Google Reader. If you find someone Tweeting about your products or a person who is looking for a solution that your product provides, let them know about you.

Use Twitter to promote new tools. Twitter users love new toys, especially if they create some sort of outcome, grade, or analysis of the person using the tool. Make the results of your tool/grader as easy to Tweet as possible. Perhaps you could add a "Tweet this grade" function. Make sure your tool is as easy to share as possible.

Establish yourself as a thought leader in your industry. By Tweeting about useful resources and thoughtful tips, you and your company will eventually develop thought leadership, and people will consider you an expert in that particular subject. Be sure to link to your own resources as well as others.

Use Twitter for Public Relations

Develop relationships with reporters, bloggers and other media people through Twitter. Reporters and big-time bloggers are incredibly active in social networks, especially when gathering information for stories.

Watch for Tweets about editorial opportunities. Because the nature of Twitter is very quick-response, it's a great place for media people to look for last-minute, additional resources for their stories. When following bloggers and reporters on Twitter, keep close track of their Tweets and scan for any opportunities.

It's also a great idea to send reporters tips to other links and resources simply to be helpful and improve your relationship with the media person, even if it's in regard to another company. The media person will be thankful for your help and more likely use you as a reference when the subject is applicable to you!

Direct message (DM) reporters or journalists instead of sending them an e-mail. By sending a direct message, you are forced to create a short concise pitch that a reporter is more likely to read. Also, direct messages are very casual. Some media folks prefer DMs to e-mail pitches. Also, it saves you the time it would normally take to write a lengthy pitch. Remember, you can only DM people if they follow you back. However, don't pitch too much. They could easily unfollow...making it much more difficult to connect.

Use Twitter to check-in on your media person before PR pitching. Check to see what the person you're about to pitch is up to before contacting them. In the event that the person is sick, having a bad day or away on travel—it may be best to contact him or her at another time.

Use Twitter for Customer Service

Respond to concerns people Tweet about your company or products. Designate a specific person in your company to track your company name and products in Twitter search. That person can address any negative comments, give feedback and help customers solve their products in real-time. The speedy response will impress the customer! Comcast at http://twitter.com/ComcastCares does a great job tracking and addressing customer concerns.

Be sure to follow back everyone who follows your company account. Although it's acceptable to pick and choose those you *want to* follow back in your personal account, there's no reason to limit those your company follows. Also, the added benefit of following back everyone who follows your company account is their ability to then DM you.

Prepping Your Twitter Marketing Message

The first thing to do is to get the URL – or Web address – of the page you want to Tweet about. Then, come up with a descriptive message about the page you are linking to.

For this you could use any number of descriptions (i.e. *A Buyer's Guide to Decorating with Candlesticks*). Make it a brief statement that will pique your follower's interest.

Shorten URLs and Track Twitter Traffic

Once you have an idea of the message you want to send out, the next step will be to take the URL of the page you will direct

Twitter users to and shorten it in length. Doing this will give you extra characters for YOUR marketing message.

In the Tweet, you can provide a direct link using a URL redirection service (more commonly called a URL shrinker). This is an online service that will assign a short URL to the page and redirect users from that shorter URL to your website.

Using our example, we would need to include the following URL in the Tweet:

http://super.really.longwebsite.com/address/about/candlesti cks.

This URL is 62 characters. By using a URL shrinker, we can change that to a 20-character URL and use those saved characters to add more meaningful details in the Tweet.

For example, the Bit.ly URL shrink service (it creates 20-character URLs) would redirect people to a shorter URL that would look something like this: http://bit.ly/12abc3.

As an added benefit, once you've found a URL shrink service you like, you can register for an account (often free) and obtain tracking information to then see how many hits the shortened URL gets. It will also track how many people on Twitter retweet your short URL.

This tracking information will be useful to help you determine which of your small business marketing messages work on Twitter – and which get ignored.

Some of the other URL redirection services you can try include Cligs (20-character URLs) and TinyURL (25-character URLs).

Put Your Message in Front of Those Who Care

Every Tweet you send as a part of your marketing strategy should be written with the goal of obtaining as much exposure as possible. This means you want people with similar interests to see your message and, hopefully, retweet it to their followers.

On Twitter, a hash tag (#) is a way of organizing your Tweets for Twitter search engines. Basically, this will allow others to search Twitter for a specific topic. If you've tagged your message with a search term, your Tweet will be seen by a larger audience with related interests.

For example, Tweets that discussed superbowl commercials used the hash tags #brandbowl. And in the below screenshot, Constant Contact (one of our FAVORITE tools) uses the hash tag #smallbusinesses.

Finalizing Your Tweet

Retweeting is crucial to maximizing your exposure, so making it easy for others to send out your marketing message is helpful.

You can encourage retweeting simply by leaving space for someone else to include the standard retweet statement without having to edit the tweet. This means you'll need to leave the number of characters in your username plus space for adding a retweet @ message.

Make a Commitment

One of the worst things a business can do is embrace their consumers in social media...and then leave them hanging. When you decide to start using Twitter for business, be sure you're ready to make a long-term commitment. Start by telling your customers and brand followers that you're on Twitter. Be transparent and friendly when you address concerns and public Tweets made to you. Make sure you Tweet messages that will encourage a direct response and comments from those following you.

Update your Twitter status every day and make sure you throw out those special links and deals to your Twitter following. Keep on consistently giving your followers a reason to stay connected to ou and reading your daily updates.

Brainstorm. What are some one-word topics that are related to your business?

LinkedIn

LinkedIn is a professional niche social networking site. On LinkedIn, you can connect with professional colleagues, meet new people, find recommended services, and find new contacts in your current network. Currently, you can reach "more than 11 million" professionals on the service, including all of the Fortune 500 companies.

What You Can Do With LinkedIn

It's important to remember that LinkedIn is a good tool to reach specific people. It's NOT so good at mass market broadcasting. If you want to reach 10 million people, then this may not be your best avenue. If, however, you want to reach the specific person who may be interested in your service, then LinkedIn can definitely be a very useful tool.

Even looking at LinkedIn from a very high-level point of view, there is much you can achieve with the service. You can see who your friends know in order to take advantage of your existing network. You can also find out "who you need to know" to reach your goals. For example, if you sell paper products, you can find out who is in charge of purchasing these supplies at the company you want to do business with.

Aside from these basic uses, there are other uses for LinkedIn. For example, by using LinkedIn effectively, you can:

- Increase the visibility of your business and brand
- Pursue direct sales
- Generate traffic and support your SEO efforts

Set Up Your Profile on LinkedIn

Setting up a LinkedIn profile is free and quick. You will receive a confirmation e-mail to activate your profile. You are then set to expand your network.

Complete your profile. Your profile should be 100% complete. Add work experience, schools, and other relevant information about yourself. People searching for contacts will make a decision to connect or not to connect based on the information you provide in your profile. A complete profile will increase your visibility and help you get found by employers, recruiters, and prospects.

Upload a profile photo. People are more likely to connect with you if they recognize your face. Plus, they feel like they are connecting with a real person.

Get recommended. Ask for recommendations from friends,

colleagues, partners, and clients. This will speak to your experience and add to your credibility in your industry.

Public Profile   http://www.linkedin.com/in/rachelbjerstedt Edit

Optimize your profile for SEO. There are two key areas that you'll want to edit so that your profile encourages search engines to find you and your company. This makes it easy for people to link to your profile or find it again if they forget exactly how they found you. And if you put your name in your profile URL, that makes it a little more SEO-friendly for searches related to your name.

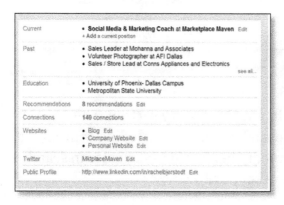

Remember how we created a username for your Facebook page and profile? We do the same thing for LinkedIn. Just like the other social networks, your profile starts with a string of random letters and

numbers. Click "Edit" and set your public profile to be your name or company (if you are setting up a company profile).

You can have up to three links on your profile to other websites. By customizing the anchor text on these links, you can rank higher for certain keywords because search engines look at the text of the links to understand more about the content of the pages they link to. Most people will leave it at the default settings (see below).

To change/optimize these, click on the 'Edit' button. In the drop down box to the right of 'Websites' select 'Other.' You'll then be given an extra box to put in your keyword title. You can fill in your website URL in the very next box. You have the ability to add up to three sites, so take advantage of this.

Optimize keywords in your summary section. This is a full text section that is indexed by Google. Including your favorite keywords in your summary helps you rank higher in search engine results for these keyword searches

Building Your Network

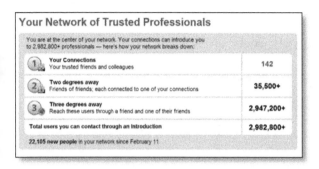

When you first sign up with LinkedIn, it may seem a little... quiet. If you only hear the echoing sound of your own voice when you sign in, it's not that there's noone using the service, it could simply be that your network is quite small.

Connect with people you've worked or done business with, or people with similar interests or who work in your industry. Invite thought leaders in your industry to connect so that you might establish a relationship with them and, eventually, gain access to their network.

Start with people you know. First reach out to friends, colleagues, relatives and business contacts as this will help you build the first layer of your network.

Find people by company. Search under the "Companies" tab so you can start looking for employees that are working in your industry. You can use this method of searching to find the contacts for the types of companies your business is trying to target.

Update your status often. Your status appears on your profile and in the LinkedIn network updates e-mailed to your connections. Thus, others may take notice of what you're working on and decide to connect or click-through on links in your status.

Connect your Twitter and LinkedIn accounts. LinkedIn now allows you to connect your Twitter account to your LinkedIn

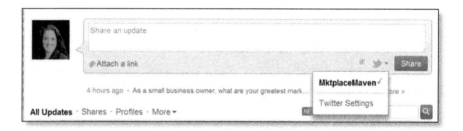

profile via your status. This feature allows you to post a LinkedIn status message to Twitter and to pull a Tweet into your LinkedIn status. Enabling this feature will help you leverage both of these networks to build connections on both sites. (You can also link Facebook to Twitter, thus forming a chain – or a domino effect – of updates.)

LinkedIn Tools

LinkedIn Answers

Basically, "Answers" is just as it sounds. Anyone can ask a question, and anyone can answer. The nice thing about this tool is that you can interact with people who are not in your network. This helps you meet new people and make new contacts.

When you ask a question in the Answers area, many people can answer you. When the question closes (automatically after a few days or when you decide to close it), you're asked to choose the "good" answers. Out of these "good" answers, you are asked to choose a "best" answer. The person who is chosen as having given the "best" answer gets an "expertise point" that shows in their LinkedIn profile.

Answers offers a great deal of opportunity to display your expertise. If someone is looking for help on a topic where you have expert knowledge, your answer not only shows what you know, it also opens a conversation with someone in need of your expertise. And if you want to keep up- to-date on what questions are being asked in your category, you can always subscribe to the RSS feed.

At the same time, asking a question can also be helpful. Your question may be read by many people who have an interest in the topic. This can be a good place to announce new ventures and look for new business partners.

> **Brainstorm**. What are some categories that are related to your business?

Search LinkedIn

The "Search" function in LinkedIn allows you to find people, regardless of if you know them or not. You then have the

option of finding someone who knows them to introduce you, purchasing a paid account from LinkedIn to contact them directly yourself, or finding another way to contact them.

LinkedIn Groups

Groups on LinkedIn are actually quite simple. By joining a group, everyone in the group basically becomes a connection. Anyone else who is also a member can see the group logo in your profile. LinkedIn recently announced a new "LinkedIn for Good" charity program. It will be interesting to see how this service develops.

Marketing Strategies

Increasing your brand's visibility. There are several ways you can use LinkedIn to increase the visibility of your business. First, you can display your expertise in Answers. Frequently, people ask questions like, "Where can I find a consultant?" or other similar questions. If you fit the bill, you can use the question to start a conversation.

Second, you can announce your services to others in Answers. Simply answer a question that relates to your service or ask a question looking for something you need.

Third, you can drive readers to your blog posts. If someone asks a question to which you have blogged the answer, simply point people to your blog post – driving traffic and gaining a quality, relevant link at the same time.

Finally, you can get your service recommended in "Services." The more recommendations you have, the better your business looks.

Supporting Your SEO

LinkedIn is actually a reasonably good, quality site to get a link from. They are also (as of this writing) NOT using the "nofollow" tag on their outgoing links.

More and more people are recognizing the need to build a network of *quality* links to their websites. Not only can these links provide a way for search engines to find you, but they can also drive qualified, relevant traffic.

If your organization has, say, 100 employees and 40 of them have LinkedIn accounts, then why not send out a company-wide e-mail requesting a link back to the company website? If only 20 staff members add a link, you're still up 20 free, quality – possibly relevant – links, simply by sending an e-mail. And remember, each account on LinkedIn has space for three links with whatever anchor text you like.

In order to make the link viewable to search engines, it's important to add the "show website" feature to each profile that will link to your site. This can be done in each account by clicking on "Edit My Public Profile." Make sure "Full View" is checked and that "Websites" are also checked. This will make the website link (and anything else you check here) public. Again, you can respond to service requests and other questions in LinkedIn Answers where you can post a link to your website as a reference. Many Answers pages are also indexed in search engine results pages.

Here are 12 ways to use LinkedIn more effectively:

1. Fill out your profile completely to earn trust. Use widgets to integrate other tools, such as importing your blog entries or Amazon books into your profile.
2. Publish your LinkedIn URL on all your marketing collateral, including business cards, e-mail signature, e-mail newsletters, web sites and brochures.
3. Grow your network by joining industry and alumni groups related to your business.
4. Research your prospects before meeting or contacting them.
5. Write honest and valuable recommendations for your contacts.
6. Request LinkedIn recommendations from happy customers willing to provide testimonials.
7. Post your presentations on your profile using a presentation application.
8. Ask your first-level contacts for introductions to their first-level contacts.
9. Interact with LinkedIn on a regular basis to reach those who may not see you on other social media sites.
10. Set up to receive LinkedIn messages in your inbox so you can respond right away.
11. Link to articles and content posted elsewhere with a summary of why it's valuable. This will add to your credibility.
12. List your newsletter subscription information and archives.

YouTube

YouTube's not just for posting silly videos of sleepwalking dogs and other embarrassing moments — it can also be used as a highly-effective business tool. You can use it to show off your expertise, share knowledge, market your products, and connect with customers, colleagues and prospects.

Getting Started on YouTube

To create a YouTube account:

- Navigate to YouTube, and click 'Create Account.'

- If you're already signed into your Google Account, you will be prompted to sign out. Do so.

- In the e-mail address field, enter the e-mail address associated with your Google Account and fill in the rest of your information.

- On the next page, you'll be prompted to sign into your Google Account. The e-mail address you entered on the previous page will pre-populate the Google account e-mail field.

- Click 'Sign In' to link your accounts and sign in to YouTube.

Once you have a YouTube user account, you will automatically have a channel. Another thing to think about is whether you want to have two different accounts. For example, we have a personal account where we can share videos of my daughter (and subscribe to videos of my nieces and nephews), but we keep that completely separate from business.

I highly recommend creating a Google account with you@yourdomainname.com. Use this for all of your Google products that are related to your business (i.e. Adwords, Adsense, Google Analytics, etc.).

Watch some videos

Search for any video or topic. Click "Browse" to explore YouTube. Choose to view results under Videos, Music, Shows, Movies or Trailers, and filter by your category of interest. Once you're on a category page, filter the results further by popularity and date range.

Found a video you like? Click Like and add it to your Favorites so you can easily find it in your account. Share it with your friends on Twitter, Facebook, or other social networks. Subscribe to receive automatic updates from the channel.

Get in the habit of sharing videos. Why? Because you'll want your clients, prospects and business partners to do the same with your videos.

Upload a video

Upload a file from your computer or record a video using your phone or webcam. You can also edit your videos right in YouTube – no software downloads required! Combine your video clips, trim the length of your video, add music, and add transitions between video clips.

For best results, complete the Settings and Info sections for your video. Include relevant keywords in the Tags section and select the appropriate category. Give the video an accurate title and description to help people discover it.

Then decide whether you need to share your video publicly or use private sharing to control who can watch it. (Perhaps you are creating user training videos that are meant exclusively for paying clients. Those would be private.)

Tip! One thing to keep in mind with your YouTube channel...don't upload 10 videos all at once and then not upload anything for the next six months. Space your videos so that your channel looks fresh. That will help you attract and retain more subscribers.

What to Post on YouTube

So now that you've gotten your account and channel set up, the next step is to start producing and posting videos. Some ideas for the types of video to produce are:

Show off your expertise and position yourself as a thought leader

- Upload recordings of presentations you've given to demonstrate authority and public speaking skills.
- Share slides from presentations that weren't recorded or create a recording directly on your desktop.
- Create short videos of valuable tips of interest to your clients and prospects to show off your expertise.
- Conduct an interview with an expert.

Small Business Case Study: Curly Kinks

Q: What made you start and promote your product line on YouTube?

A: There were a few reasons why I decided to create my own product line. I was spending hundreds of dollars each month searching for products that performed the way I wanted them to. I finally got tired of doing that and decided to come up with my own line [Natural Hair Care Line]. I also saw there was a market for natural hair care products that catered to the very tightly coiled, natural kinky hair types [very similar to mine]. So my line was created out of necessity for me and my four girls who are also natural.

Q: When you first started YouTube did you understand its vastness?

A: When I first started YouTube I really didn't [realize] how big it truly was. I didn't know there was this enormous natural hair community [seeking tips and instruction]. I saw a few videos that inspired me to document my own natural journey and from my first initial video I received an overwhelming amount of support and subscribers [which lead me to continue to make more videos].

Q: How often did you/do you post a video? Do you notice a correlation in number of posting and number of new subscribers?

A: When I first started it was about 2-3 videos a month, sometimes more. I didn't really keep track of how many subscribers I had because I didn't notice until it was well over a few hundred. I would check every few months and each time I checked it had grown by a couple hundred. I now have over 11,000 subscribers [as of September 2011], and it is still growing.

Q: Do you have any tips for success for YouTube?

A: I would say be yourself! Don't be like anyone else or copy what someone else is doing. People like to see variety, and they can tell when you are being fake. So always be real and be yourself. Make your videos about something that you know people want to watch! Also, keep in contact with your subscribers and update them at least once a month!

Q: How should one get started, and with what expectation, to see success with YouTube?

A: Watch a few people you subscribe to, find out what types of videos are popular and blend that with something you are passionate about. It could be cooking, hair, art, music, etc. Make an intro video introducing yourself to your audience and what you intend to do with your channel, then go from there. It is also a good idea to take requests, ask your subscribers what they want to see and make videos based on those requests. Don't expect your videos to become hits right away. It takes time to build a following, but as long as you continue to make videos and stay in the public's view with great videos, you will get more popular as time goes on.

Interested in learning more about Curly Kinks?

Check out their YouTube Channel at:

http://www.YouTube.com/CurlyKinksProducts

Or their website at:

http://curlykinks.com/

Marketing and Advertising

- Set up a channel to reflect your brand and engage with others.
- Put together a creative video explaining your product or service.
- Show your product in action using movie trailer-style: fast, creative and catchy.
- Show the results of someone using your services.

Customer Service

- Create "how to" videos to help your customers use your product or service.
- Post solutions to common product or service problems.
- Answer customer-specific questions using videos. Imagine how surprised a customer will be when you point them to a video with the answer!
- Embed videos on your web site on appropriate pages, including customer support and product tours.

Creating High-Quality Content

Once you've gotten an idea, then plan your shoot, grab a camcorder, and...you're off! Of course, getting good raw footage is the most important concern. Tips on taking good video are all over the Web, and YouTube itself has gathered a lot of good information.

Pay attention to production value

You're not trying to win an Oscar, but your videos should be professional and easy to watch. Shaky hand-held camera work, poor audio quality, bad lighting, or lack of coherence in the story all lead to viewers changing the virtual channel. Pay attention to the lighting. Use a tripod to create smooth viewing experience. Use microphones and pay attention to the audio. Try to tell a story or clearly walk viewers through the video and what you're doing. By paying attention to these basics you'll standout from the massive amounts of poor-quality content on the site – earning you more attention and more interest from viewers.

Editing your video

You do not have to have an expensive video editing suite for YouTube. Video Editor is a free tool in your YouTube account which allows you to edit various clips and produce an entirely new edited video. In Video Editor, you can:

- Combine multiple videos you've uploaded to create a new longer video
- Trim the beginning and / or end of your videos
- Add a soundtrack from YouTube's AudioSwap library
- Create new videos without worrying about file formats, and publish the new video to YouTube with one click (no new upload is required)

To get started, login to your YouTube account and go to Video Editor (www.youtube.com/editor).

> **Tip!** Go the extra mile by adding closed-captions or subtitles to your videos. Remember that not everyone can watch or hear videos in the same way.

If you're editing your video on your desktop, save your video in the appropriate format for YouTube. They recommend the following settings for the best presentation:

- You should always upload your video in the original format and in the highest quality possible.
- YouTube prefers de-interlaced files.
- If your file is using h264 encoding, they prefer files without PAFF/MBAFF encoding.
- Audio and video lengths should be the same and audio should begin at the same time as the video.

You can find these settings in your editing software's "save as," "render as" or "export" options.

YouTube restrictions

YouTube does impose some restrictions. For regular accounts, videos must be less than 100MB in size and 10 minutes in length. For longer corporate presentations and events, you must include only the highlights or break them into separate videos. Or, you can apply for a "Partner" account that allows you to post videos longer than 10 minutes as well as additional customization option and advertising commissions.

For some videos, like corporate projects or client training, you may want to mark the video as "Private." That way, only the people you specify in a contact list can see it. YouTube accounts automatically provide "Friends" and "Family" contact lists, but you can also make your own. After your video is marked as "Private" and uploaded, you can watch it in the YouTube player and simply click on the "Share Video" link, choose the list you want to share it with and click the "Send" button.

Optimize for YouTube search

Nearly 24 hours of new video is uploaded to YouTube every minute of every day. In order to be found, you need to *optimize your video* so that it can be found on the site. Here are just a few things to think about when adding your video to YouTube:

Include important keywords in the title, and be sure your tags include those keywords as well.

Choose an appealing thumbnail that clearly depicts what your video is about.

If you're a plumber, you may want to title your video "How to fix a leaky toilet. XYZ Plumbing top tips for fixing a leaky toilet." Your tags might be "how to, toilet, toilets, leaky toilets, running toilet, plumbing, DIY," etc. The thumbnail could be a shot of you holding the flushing mechanism (assuming that YouTube gives you that as an option). Your title, keywords and thumbnail all gives your viewers the information they need to decide whether your video will help meet their need and solve their problem.

Give the viewers a follow-up action

You want to create a desire for viewers to take a follow-up action. If you've created an informational video about fixing leaking toilets, you want to give the viewer a compelling reason to follow-up with you and a clear path to do so. One way to do this is to provide a special offer and a unique web address in the video.

For example, a call-to-action such as "Print step-by-step instructions and receive 10% off our in-home evaluation by visiting MySite.com/YouTube" gives your viewers an actionable next step with clear value. The unique URL and discount will also provide you one measurable way to determine how successful your YouTube video is.

Let them know who you are

Don't be afraid to create awareness about who you are and what you do. It's important to let people know who they're getting this valuable information from. You should encourage users to take a step towards a relationship with your company by having them subscribe to your YouTube channel or company e-mail newsletter (if you have one). By building your YouTube subscriber base, you'll automatically reach a built-in audience of potential customers who have opted-in to seeing your latest videos.

Our plumber in the above example could say "Subscribe to our YouTube channel for more moneysaving tips on how to eliminate leaks around your home" and include that call-to-action graphically in the video.

Blogs

The argument for blogging is all around us. We may know a blogger or two. We may know a dozen or a hundred bloggers. And among those we know we find that many are blogging for business purposes. Whether it's the hobbyist who just wants to make a few cents off Google AdSense or the enterprise social media company that has elected to launch a blog to showcase its expertise in expansive applications, blogging is an affordable way for individuals and companies alike to become a respected voice in an increasingly competitive online environment.

What do blogs do for your business? Like all other means of social media promotion, blogs can:

- Establish thought leadership.
- Increase traffic to websites since bloggers can optimize for keywords using search engine optimization techniques that will help customers find the business or product that they need.
- Help build links to corporate web sites. This helps people find your business in online searches.
- Build brand awareness. This gets your business known globally or wherever you are looking to be found.

The boom of weblogs happened in 1999 when several companies and developers made easy blogging software and tools. Since 1999, the number of blogs on the Internet has exploded from a few thousand to over 100 million.

Blogs can fall into two general categories:

- Personal Blogs: A mixture of a personal diary, opinion posts, and research links.
- Business Blogs: A corporate tool for communicating with customers or employees to share knowledge and expertise.

Business blogs are sweeping the business community. Blogs are an excellent method to share a company's expertise, build additional web traffic, and connect with potential customers.

What to Blog About

Blogging is not only good to interact with your market, but can be a good, less pressured platform to promote your products from. A blog tends to be a less formal atmosphere, so it lets people put their guard down. You can do some "soft selling" on a blog. Write a post about a topic, then promote a product that can help your readers on that same topic. For example: if you write a blog about dog training, give them a great training tip and then promote a training collar.

But I'm Not a Writer...

Blog posts can take many forms. They don't always have to be long-form essays. They can be:

- A bulleted list
- One photo with a caption
- Several photos with captions
- A comic strip
- A review of a book, a film, a product
- A How-To guide
- A How-NOT-To guide

- A short video
- A short audio clip
- An interview
- A profile
- A rant
- A rave
- A thoughtful response to somebody else's blog post

And the list goes on. Sometimes you just don't have an essay-form post in you. And frankly, sometimes your audience can't stomach another wordy post. Grab a striking photo from your file of pictures or your Flickr photo stream, post it, and write a line or two about it. Record a short video using your webcam and post it on YouTube or Viddler so that you can easily embed it on your blog.

Three Quick Blogging Tips

Always be ready. Carry a small notebook with you so that you can jot down ideas for topics when they come to you. You might be at the playground with your kids or at the gas station and something will pop into your head. If you wait until you get home, the idea may be gone forever.

Write a series. Choose a popular topic and write a series on it, lasting a week or a month. That way, you know what you will write about each time and it makes coming up with content much easier.

Invite guest bloggers. This is not something you want to do all the time, as it is *your* blog and you want your readers to get to know you. But from time to time, it can be helpful to

---

you and fun for your readers to hear from someone else. Make sure they write about things that your readers are interested in.

What Does Blogging Provide to Small Business?

Blog software is easy to use. Simply write your thoughts, link to resources, and publish to your blog, all at the push of a few buttons. Blog software companies such as Movable Type, Blogger.com, and TypePad all offer easy blogging tools to get started. Other blog software companies (like WordPress...also known as Content Management Systems) can manage your entire website.

Business blogs provide your small business with a chance to share your expertise and knowledge with a larger audience. And this is a powerful benefit for consultants and knowledge workers.

Why blog for promotions?

Blogging is very popular right now. And having a business blog that provides good information for your customers while also being timely and fun can add a new dimension to your Web site.

Blogs are a powerful tool for marketing and promotion. Because the entries are short and often full of links, they're more keyword-heavy than standard articles. Plus, because they're shorter, they are easy for your customers to read (and you to write). People are more likely to come back daily to see what you might have to say on that day.

If your company is very formal, a blog is a place to show your customers that it's made up of people just like them. You can do this without becoming too personal or diary-like.

How to Use a Blog for Business

FAQs

If you get a lot of mail to your Webmaster account, you can post the common questions on a blog. This will provide your customers a place to go and see questions and answers. As new questions come in, you can post them to help more people.

Contests

Daily contests and games are a great promo on a blog. They are fun and bring your customers back. Queensboro Shirt Company often has haiku contests on their blog – they give the winner free products.

What's new?

If you add lots of new articles, information, or products regularly, sometimes it can be difficult for your customers to find out what's new. A quick blog entry can show them what's updated on your site.

What's coming?

You can use a blog to peak interest in future products or projects. It's also a great way to keep notes about what you're planning for your customers. The entries are archived so nothing is lost either for you or your customers. Plus, if your blog tool has a comments feature, you can use that to judge interest before it goes live.

Starting a Blog

A corporate blog provides a forum for your company's leaders and employees to discuss topics of interest with your prospects, customers, and the people who influence them. A corporate blog can consist of several individual blogs, each written by different employees ("specialists"). It can also have a summary company blog that incorporates all of the individual blogs.

Organizing a blog in this fashion creates many more opportunities for your company to be found online and to generate new business.

So, how do you get everyone in your organization on board?

> **Tip: If you have a larger company, appoint a blogging administrator. Dedicate a specific resource to manage the blog. This person's top responsibilities will include:**
>
> - Monitoring that everyone submits his/her blog posts on the assigned day.
> - Keeping everyone excited about blogging.
> - Making sure those subject matter experts are involved to review posts in their areas of expertise.

Step One: Commit

Write a weekly post or delegate this task to some of your more creative employees. If you have a whole office staff, get your whole team onboard. Ask every employee to write a short blog once a week or biweekly.

Everyone should be enthusiastic about blogging. You can't assume, however, that everyone will communicate in a way that your readers will easily understand.

Develop an editorial calendar

Determine how you want to document your calendar. This could be a spreadsheet, document, Google calendar, physical calendar, or even a WordPress plugin!

Brainstorm content ideas and decide how you want to distribute them. Do you want to rotate through various topics, focus on a topic each week, or even create a weekly column (i.e. Thankful Thursday)? Once you decide, try to stay consistent so your audience (and future sponsors) knows what to expect.

Consider holiday and topical posts to include.

Move things around if they don't fit! This is why it helps to use an online tool at first.

Don't be afraid to add additional content on top of your editorial calendar posts. Depending on your blog topic, timely information may need to be included. You can slot in a generic spot for news-focused posts, or add them in on top of your planned content.

Write For Your Target Audience

You might know everything there is to know about the internal system dynamics of combustion engines in aeronautic vehicles, but that doesn't mean your audience will understand a word you just said. (Yes, I made up that example, and I am sure there isn't such a thing!)

Before you start blogging, you need to determine and personalize your target audience. Speak their language. Think: Who are you writing to? Who do you want to read your blogs? Visualize the answers.

Have a Plan to Market Your Blog Content

Search engine optimization (commonly referred to as SEO) has its roots in efforts by Webmasters to make their Websites easy to access and crawl by search engines. The concept has been evolving into something much bigger and broader than simply making Websites "crawlable" by the machines. SEO has started to cover usability issues, conversion tactics, backlink acquisition, and more. Most SEO experts, including Google engineers, agree that the blog is an area that holds great leverage in all aspects of SEO.

Remember: Search bots only "see" text and keywords. They are straightforward and, well, they are machines.

Your primary task is to make your blog easy to understand and interpret even for those robots. Three basics:

- Create a clear navigation and naturally link to your old content and posts.
- Create natural keyword prominence: Have your important words in the "prominent" places.
- Make your pages lightweight for people and bots to load easily. (Hint: No Flash!!).

SEO Terms That All Bloggers Should Know

Title tag <title> aka the Title of the Post

The title of each post is of crucial importance. Not only will it grab your readers' attention and prompt them to read further, the page title is also the most "prominent" place to showcase your important keywords:

- Title tags are displayed in search results (this is the linked part of Google search engine listing).

- Title tags are used by search bots to "understand" the main topic of the page.

Make sure to create catchy and attention-grabbing titles AND include some post-specific details in them. Helpful details might include the product you are reviewing, the person you are interviewing, the place you are describing, or the market you are covering. These "details" can help to get your post to appear in relevant searches.

Some best practices and rules:

- All titles throughout the site should be unique (do not use the same title for more than one blog post).

- Title tags should be preferably no longer than 70 characters (including spaces).

- Page titles should be specific and contain your main keyword(s) to help Googlebot understand what the page is about.

Meta Description

Officially, the meta description is not taken into account for ranking websites. It IS used to generate the search snippet (those couple of lines you see below the linked part on the search results page). Meta descriptions should be attention-grabbing and concise. They are a great opportunity to exert control on the text that searchers will see when your posts come up in queries.

URL Structure

Clear, "readable" URL structure will help with both the usability and SEO of your blog:

- URLs containing keywords will appear in search results (with keywords in bold).
- Search engines take keywords in the URL into account to rank web pages in search results.

Avoid very long URLs. No more than 3-5 words in your URL. Avoid uppercase in URLs. And remember that the URL is case sensitive.

PINTEREST

There's no time like the present to take advantage of Pinterest, the blistering-hot, new, graphics-based social media, to help grow and market your business. (Users: 70% female.)

The most important reason has nothing to do with Pinterest itself and everything to do with:

- What's trending now
- Facebook's Edge rank algorithm

Understanding Pinterest's Peculiar Power

Facebook has created a new algorithm that that focuses on three post or comment elements:

- Media used – Graphic or text? Video? Link?
- Affinity – How relevant is the post to the Facebook poster's Friends and followers?
- Time Decay – How old is the post? (The further back in time, the less relevant)

But don't kid yourself: out of these criteria, Facebook's overwhelming favorite is "Media used".

And out of all the media you could possibly use, Facebook wants photos attached to your posts; or photos shared as posts. (Graphic illustrations too, if you treat them like photos.)

Why?   Here's your answer...

That's right. Facebook is using the photos you post to serve up paid advertisements and "Sponsored Stories".

It weights Pinterest posts exactly like photos – but if a reader clicks on a Pinterest photo in Facebook, not only do they have the option within Facebook to re-"Share" the photo, they are transported immediately to the poster's actual Pinterest Pinboard...

...Where once again they are invited to share the Pin on Facebook and Twitter, gaining maximum weight for both Facebook and Pinterest.

But wait – *Google* loves Pinterest too!

If you have a strong LinkedIn or Facebook presence, you'll most likely see links from those URLs, if you search for your own name (E.G.: "Gerry Smith") in Google Search...

...But if you don't have a strong profile on Facebook, Pinterest will almost instantly vault your name to the top of Google search results – providing you with instant social proof and respectability!

(The Facebook friend whose name I used for the example, above, has been an inhabitant of Facebook for years, but she is not a marketer and has done nothing that would vault her to the top of the search results – except recently join Pinterest and make a few cross-posts between Pinterest and Facebook!)

So now that you're beginning to get a glimmer of how quickly Pinterest can position you far ahead of peers, let's apply some of this heft to your marketing...

Setting Up a Profile on Pinterest

Here's another "trick" about Pinterest you need to know...

If you go directly to the Pinterest home page to "Request an Invite" (a.k.a. join), you may wait several precious days before they send you an acceptance letter.

To sign up and be allowed access quickly, simply:

1. **Check your Facebook Page and look for Pinterest posts**. If you don't know the difference between a personal photo and what is a Pinterest post, here's a quick way to find one: Look for those graphics-with-quotes that are so popular nowadays! (Hint: Take note of the quote graphics … after you get started you can make some of your own!)

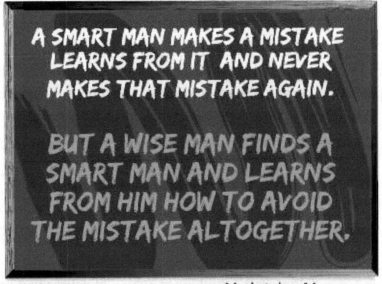

A SMART MAN MAKES A MISTAKE LEARNS FROM IT AND NEVER MAKES THAT MISTAKE AGAIN.

BUT A WISE MAN FINDS A SMART MAN AND LEARNS FROM HIM HOW TO AVOID THE MISTAKE ALTOGETHER.

www.MarketplaceMaven.com

2. Direct Message the friend posting the quote and ask her to send you a Pinterest invitation!

3. When you receive her response, click on the link and go through the signup process. There won't be a delay.

Start Pinning!

When you go through the sign-up process – which is so easy, you won't have any problems following the Wizard – be sure to select several suggested (human) posters and boards you think you'll not only like, but will be aligned to your business interests (I.E.: Relevant!)

Before you leave that page, scroll right down to the bottom and de-select any suggested Friends (imported from your other Social Networks) whose interests might dilute your marketing focus. (Don't worry: They won't know.)

Now create about **five Pinboards of your own** – all relevant to your niche topic or niche group's interest – but not try not to do any blatant marketing. Remember – social media is about conversation – not salesmanship.

(Don't let the idea of creating Pinboards intimidate you: You can get away with as little as one photo per board – just try to make sure it's any one or more of the following:

- An eye-catching stunner
- Visually gorgeous
- Shocking (but not negative or in violation of Pinterest's guidelines, which of course you have read)
- Curiosity-arousing
- Emotion-triggering
- Uplifting

Now start sharing your Pins on Facebook and Twitter (particularly Facebook). Make sure you make a daily habit of Liking, Re-pinning and Commenting on other peoples' relevant Pins and Pinboards. (Subscribe to them, too – but be selective! Let "relevancy" be your watchword.)

Make it Easy for People to Connect with You

Just like your other social media icons, place "Follow Me on Pinterest" Buttons on all your websites and blogs.

Pinterest has a "Goodies" page that generates code or html that you can embed on your website. If you go the Goodies page and scroll down, you'll come across the web form (below); you'll find code already generated beside the top button. You can also select instead the alternate icon choices shown here. All you do is copy-paste the generated snippet of code to your website.

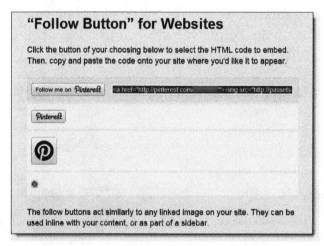

Interact with other Pinners

Add other Pinners' photos to your own boards by using "Add+" on your main horizontal menu bar from within Pinterest: Or by re-pinning a Pin (photo).

You can "suggest" to your website or blog readers that they pin your website or blog photos by installing a "Pin it Button". (Code generator also on the Goodies page, just below the "Follow me on Pinterest" generator.)

And for lightning-fast ease, add the "Pin It" button to your browser Bookmarks bar so you can lift photos and graphics from websites for sharing.

Pinterest's Help section is probably the simplest, clearest and best organized on the web: you really don't want to miss reading up on, before you start getting heavily into Pinterest. (And it won't take long!)

Create Great Pinboards

Showing bit.ly links on each pin to tell you how and where to download the mobile eBooks it pictures, this Pinboard by Jiru Lin has gathered 318 followers and 25 pins so far. (Take notes for your own  Pinterest marketing practices!) This is by no means the only Pinboard called "Mobile Marketing". There are more, containing many examples of how (and how not) to do things on Pinterest, when it comes to marketing. Comparing these can be a real learning curve, take the time to check these and other marketing-related boards out for instant, visual tips you can print out – and use.

If you decide to use Pinterest to drive your customers to your own eBooks or websites in a similar way, there are a couple of things to take into advisement:

- Make sure the site you send them to delivers **exactly what your pin promises**
- Make sure the site you send them to delivers **high value**
- Make sure the site you send them to gives them **information on Pinterest** – even your own Pinterest practices. (People who find your marketing links may be looking to see "how she did that".)
- **Put your "Follow me on Pinterest" button on your site** – as well as "Pin It" buttons for your graphics, if you don't mind them being re-pinned

Putting Pinterest to Use in Countless Ways

The more you learn about Pinterest, the more you can tailor your Pinterest use and Pinboards to your marketing goals. Do brainstorm and jot out a **Pinterest marketing strategy** before you go hog-wild with creating Pinboards. Taking this step in advance will help you decide which of the varied (and not always related) options and features to use.

Above all, make sure you thoroughly understand how features that seem parallel to those on other networks (.e.g. Hashtags,

"@") actually work on Pinterest. Assumptions are dangerous because some features are not actually similar at all; and things on this still-experimental social sharing place are not always what they seem.

Below, you'll find a smorgasbord of potentially useful tactics and tips. Select the ones you think will benefit your Pinterest marketing strategy the best – and get started!

Here are ten excellent suggestions from Edelman Digital's "Digital Sharing: Infographics" Pinboard. (Search for it on Pinterest)

1. Create a themed group board for your niche
2. Pin client images
3. Create a group scavenger hunt of pins
4. Host a Pinboard tour
5. "Throw a Pinterest Party!"
6. Monthly Pinboard Contest
7. "Make infographic text LARGE"
8. "Let your personality shine"
9. Focus on lifestyle, not product
10. Include keywords in each Pinboard description

Above all, run Searches on Pinterest and pay attention to what your fellow Pinners are doing! Take things you like and adapt them to your own marketing models (and be sure to check Pinterest guidelines first, to see if what you're doing is "legal"!)

Add Pinterest to your Facebook Timeline

Be sure to add Pinterest to your Facebook Timeline, to make it easier for people to access your Pins. Here's now:

1. Log into your Pinterest account

2. Click your Username (top-right toolbar)

3. In the page that opens up, click the "Edit Profile" button

4. Slide down to the "Facebook" section. Click the red slider to "ON" (if it isn't already on)

5. Select who you want to be able to share your Pins with in the pop-up window that opens up. (Remember: The broader the category you pick, the more people you'll reach – but keep in mind that they may not necessarily be the most targeted)

6. Remember to click the red "Save Profile" button at the bottom of the page

(You can also do this with Twitter and Search engines.)

Host a Pinterest "Pintalk" – Pinterest is still relatively new and many people really want to know the best ways to use it. Once you're comfortable with it (which won't take long), contact a marketing talk show host and offer to have a

"Pintalk" (or whatever name you want to give it). Volunteer yourself as her special guest, and invite viewers to have questions ready. (You can also do this with your own webinar or teleseminar, if you're used to either of these media.)

For best success...

- Pick a strong topic with a single theme.

- Invite your potential audience to submit questions beforehand... so you're well-prepared and have a better idea of what they're looking for within your "Pintalk" framework

Create a "Pinterest FAQ" Page

No matter what your niche topic, add a "Pinterest FAQ" page to your blog offering tips, tricks and simple "how to" information. This social platform is new enough that Pinterest tips can vault you up in Google search rankings...

...And be sure to take a screen shot of your Pinterest FAQ page and upload it (with link displayed) to its own separate board (or one of your existing ones you feel it will make the perfect addition to.)

Invite others to add their own "Pinterest FAQ" pins.

Enable Your Pinterest Email Settings

Pinterest automatically creates a link to the email account you signed up with... but in order to enable it and specify customized options such as notification if someone has re-pinned your photo or followed you, you'll need to indicate this and choose your preferences.

1. Click on your Profile photo

2. Choose "Edit Profile button"

3. Choose "Change Email Settings button

4. Select the options you want

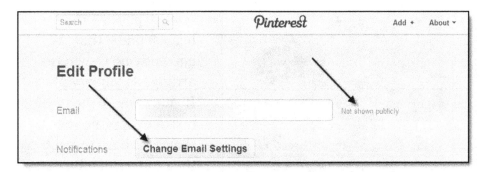

Be sure to specify who can see your email address and/or contact you. The last thing you want is to be unaware that you've accidentally set or left your email setting status as "not shown publicly".

(Make sure you enable Pinterest "News" emails. This is the easiest and simplest way to receive advance notice on the latest changes and updates.)

Make Full Use of Pinterest Descriptions

You have up to 500 characters with which to create engaging, interesting, fascinating and clear descriptions.

Use your best **keywords** and – as always – do your best to grab the viewer's attention. (Best way? Make your pin resonate emotionally so they relate it to their own lifestyle or experiences.)

Rearranging Your Pinboard

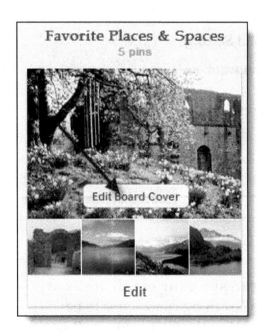

Although you can "Set Board Cover" and choose a particular photo ("pin") in each Pinboard as the fixed "cover" photo – the biggest one – there is currently no way to re-arrange secondary pins. If you want all pins in a board to appear, you therefore have to limit the number of pins per board to five. Any more than that particular number and you may want to consider creating a new Pinboard.

Remember that your latest pin will always appear FIRST (left-hand position) in your Pinboard... so save the most important secondary pin to last.

Tag Pins to Specific Pinterest Users

You can easily tag a Pin to a specific user by using the "@" sign in front of their Pinterest username. The only drawback is that, currently, they won't be notified specifically that you've done this.

Use Hashtags

One of the most wonderful things you can do with Pinterest is to create Pinterest hashtags! (Put them in your Descriptions.)

Do so, and use them. But be aware that Pinterest hashtags more like keyword search assistance, rather than like Twitter hashtags.

And be aware that hashtags are clickable! When you do click on a Hashtag in a Description, you will be taken to a random selection of pins containing that particular keyword.

Focus on your customers and clients

It's easy to get carried away pinning photos and graphics that you like on your Pinboards. After all, that's what Pinterest's main mission encourages at every step!

But remember that the purpose of your Pinterest Pinboards is slanted towards your potential customers or clients. Before you start pinning, take the time to research and identify...

- Their dreams
- Their interests
- Their goals
- Their values
- Their ideals
- Their truths
- Their lifestyles

If you include pictures of your products, make those pictures **relevant to your intended viewer**. Don't just show them

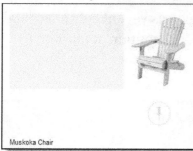

Muskoka Chair

your product... Show them your product being used in a setting they would likely use it in. (For example, your custom-made Muskoka chair idyllically arranged in a setting that triggers ideas on how to use Muskoka chairs at their own weekend cottage.

As a character in a novel I recently read wisely commented on selling: "It's all about the sizzle – not the sausage."

Pinterest Search

Don't underestimate the Pinterest search function, either. Not only can you make sure people find you easily by thoroughly understanding its capacities (and how people use it), you can also quickly search for valuable information you, yourself, need. You can Search by: Pins, Boards or People

---

The Truth about Affiliate Marketing and Pinterest –

Finally, be aware that although you can add prices to products you post and send people to landing pages if you wish, you cannot post affiliate links to large online retail networks such as Amazon.

The reason?
Pinterest will automatically insert _its own affiliate links_ to Amazon for the product you are recommending. (Yes. Pinterest makes money from your boards!)

There is some speculation, however – as yet entirely anecdotal – that Pinterest does favor boards that contain at least one Amazon product.

---

6 Things NOT to do on Pinterest

1. **Play Nice!** Pinterest's 70% female audience loves uplifting and visually beautiful content, as previously mentioned. A hard, aggressive tone to your Pinboards or negative graphics will be utterly counter-productive.

2. **Credit Your Sources!** Pinterest itself will do this for you, most of the time – but do edit your Pins – fill in descriptions and tags – to give extra credit where credit is due.

3. **Don't lift content from websites that have disabled Pinterest-saving** Yes, you can be sneaky and use screen capture software to lift these photos anyway – but why would you want to, if the owner has made it clear they do not appreciate sharing? You'll only get yourself banned from Pinterest, if a complaint is made.

4. **Be very careful about sharing copyrighted images.** (The safest way to make sure you won't step on anyone's toes or endanger their online livelihoods is to simply share only from sites that have a "Follow me on Pinterest" or "Pin it" button for their images... or from other Pinterest Pinboards – and, of course, you can always upload your own images!)

5. **Don't lose your focus.** Keep relevant. Use keywords. Please Pinterest by sticking to its mandates and mission.

6. **Don't stick only with suggested board categories and names from Pinterest.** Create your own – based on your keywords.

LINKING THEM ALL TOGETHER

Your ultimate goal is to combine your social media approach. When someone asks a question in Twitter, respond in detail on LinkedIn and link to it from Twitter. Tweet about your contest on Facebook inviting your Twitter followers to participate.

However, social media platforms are meant for different purposes, so don't *always* post the same content *all* the time on *all* the platforms. Each audience is different and therefore should be treated as such. Remember to keep synergy between your social media profiles so that your brand is consistent but not repetitive. Advertise your social media platforms on your website, your business cards, and in your e-mail marketing.

Step One: Do Not Forget Your USP!

(Write it down below...yes, again.)

Remember that this is going to be the basis for all your communication. This USP has to resonate in each and every post. This doesn't mean that you repeat this post over and over – it means that you commit to it. Take advantage of this opportunity to really set yourself apart from your competition. Post reasons why you are different. Blog about your differences. Write a newsletter about your differences and post links to both on Twitter and Facebook.

Step Two: Develop Your Strategy & Write It Down!

Know your business. Did we mention that you need a USP? Use this to bring your brand story to life in a compelling, authentic and personal way.

Know your customers. Who are they? How will they want to connect with your brand? What content will be important to them and what will engage them?

Know your goals. What kind of relationship do you want to have with your customers? In addition to building your brand, defining and prioritizing your goals will help you create your social media strategy.

Example Strategy Plan for Sam's Market Café

ABOUT US

Sam's Market Café is a unique community destination for ultra-premium prepared foods, free-range & grass fed meats, and poultry, organic and local produce, whole grain baked goods, and natural soaps and candles.

OUR BRAND

We offer the very best quality locally sourced products and we take great pride in our personal relationships with both our customers and our vendors. We're really passionate about natural, whole foods, and we LOVE to share our discoveries.

OUR CUSTOMERS

We want to market to families of all shapes and sizes, however more than likely our target will be moms – as they make the majority of health and grocery decisions. Our store has a hippie-granola vibe and therefore we believe we will attract the natural mom – one who wants to avoid pesticides and chemicals.

OUR GOALS

We want to build connections and engage our customers on our Facebook page and inspire them to shop in our store at least three times per week. Our Twitter mission is to drive traffic to both our Facebook page and to our website. We will post excerpts from our blog on Twitter at least 3-4 times a day. We want to position ourselves as Organic Evangelists. We want to spread the word of healthful eating to our metroplex.

OUR PLAN:

- Facebook Postings: 2x/day
- Twitter Postings: 3-4 /day

> - LinkedIn Group Discussions: 2x per week
> - Blog Posts: 2 per week

Step Three: Create an Editorial Calendar

An editorial calendar is used by bloggers, publishers, and businesses to plan publication of content.

When we wrote this step, we were being presumptuous and assumed that you already created your social profiles. So, if you have not done so, create:

- ✓ Facebook Personal Profile
- ✓ Facebook Business Page
- ✓ Twitter Profile
- ✓ Blog Account (We recommend that this be embedded into your website, but you can still blog if this is a challenge for you.)
- ✓ YouTube Account

Once your accounts are created, brainstorm and figure out what you want to offer your fans, friends, and followers. Give them a reason to follow. Remember that you need to enter into a strategy with clear purpose. If you do not have a purpose, you will not receive a clear result.

Example:

Texas REALTOR®, Wayne Warshawsky, created a Facebook page called "365 Things to Do in Collin County." His approach was different than local competition. His goal and priority was first to create and build a sharing community as opposed to broadcasting his name.

The Content Creation Process

Each type of content has its own creation process and an editorial calendar helps you accommodate and plan your content. Content ideas usually are created through brainstorming based on current events, Google Alerts, industry-specific tips, and other sources.

Reminder: Consistently Contribute!

There's no point in creating a social media strategy if you are not going to be able to create content on a REGULAR basis. Your followers will not stay engaged if you do not provide relevant material. Things you can post:

- -Links to YOUR eNewsletter
- -Links to your blog
- -LinkedIn questions & answers
- -Links to other relevant eNewsletters
- -Links to articles
- -Retweet other peoples updates
- -Polls/Questions

Tools used to create an editorial calendar can vary from a notebook to computer software. You can use any of the following:

- Pieces of paper and a file folder
- A paper calendar or online calendar (for example, Google Calendar)

- A spreadsheet or online spreadsheet (i.e Excel or Google Docs).

No matter how you organize your editorial content, you will want to identify Story/Blog/Status Update Ideas and Content Production Calendar.

Step Four: Tell People

It doesn't matter what platform you start with – you will not get any friends, likes, or followers if you do not TELL people. One of the easiest things to do – especially as a small (local) business owner – is to send out an e-mail to your current clients, prospects, and networking acquaintances.

This is the e-mail that we sent...

Dear <insert name>,

Hi! I wanted to drop you a quick note to tell you about my new social media community. Yes, that's right! I have jumped on the bandwagon, and I want to invite you to join me.

Please join me on Facebook (or Twitter / YouTube) and "Like" my page.

www.Facebook.com/MarketplaceMaven*

Regards,

Rachel & Olivia

(*Of course, you would insert YOUR link! This part is easy, just copy and paste it from the URL bar from your browser.)

Do NOT be discouraged if you start with only 25 – 50 fans. It takes time to build an online community. Keep posting...and we'll see you online!

About the Authors

Marketplace Maven is a complete turnkey marketing firm that specializes in small-businesses just like yours; we are like a Swiss-army-knife for all of your marketing, PR, and communication needs.

We believe that the best way to build & grow a small business is to get noticed by your local community and your target market. If you stand out then you stay top-of-mind and subsequently sell more.

Therefore, you have a choice. Stick to the traditional, safe marketing strategies that you have always known, (You know-the strategies that your competitors are using) or employ a unique approach with a combination of inbound marketing tools and conventional marketing strategies.

We use in-house creative and technical talent as well as hand-picked vendors to offer full-service marketing and branding services. Our design and marketing services include:

- Brand Marketing & Development
- Website Development & Design
- Internet Marketing Strategies
- Graphic Design & Logo Creation
- Copywriting & Content Marketing
- Social Media Campaign Management
- Small Business Marketing & Coaching
- Marketing Strategy & Positioning

Rachel Bjerstedt

Rachel founded Marketplace Maven in 2008 after a career in advertising and media sales. Her passion is to help small business owners discover new ways to spread their "word" and create blue oceans. *(Blue Oceans? Sound Bizarre? Want to know what a Blue Ocean is and why you would want one? Then go check out the Marketplace Maven Website and read through their Marketing Tips)* Rachel has an undergraduate degree in Screenwriting and an MBA in Marketing. She is currently working towards her Doctorate in Business Administration and hopes to study small business marketing for her dissertation.

Rachel eats sleeps, and breaths, ideas. New perspectives on familiar challenges invigorate her. When she doesn't have her head buried in Seth Godin's latest book, you might be able to find her behind a camera or a paintbrush.

Olivia Myles

Olivia joined Marketplace Maven as a managing partner in 2011. She has a passion for the juxtaposition of psychology, business, and communication. Olivia's background in fashion design enables her to truly understand the importance of a first impression and encourages her obsession with brand image. Her approach to marketing is social; the more people know and like you (and your brand) the more they will buy from you.

Her education background is in business, communications, emerging media and psychology. Her Undergraduate Degree is Interdisciplinary Studies from the University of Texas at Dallas.

Still need help?

We will review your social media plan over the phone(or Skype) in a FREE 30-minute social media consultation session.

We will set up an appointment with you and carve out 30 minutes of our time to work directly with you to see your social media plan come to life. Follow the steps outlined in this book and then **shoot us an email at SocialMediaGPS@MarketplaceMaven.com.**

Or post questions on our Facebook Wall or direct message us on twitter (@MktplaceMaven) and we will do our best to answer any thing you throw at us. *(However, we still do not know the air speed velocity of any type of Barn-Yard Swallow ☺)*

JOIN THE MARKETPLACE MAVEN MASTERMIND CLUB

With the publishing of this book we have officially launched our Maven Mastermind Club! Basically it's a monthly insider's circle and eCoaching program. **Member Benefits Include:**

- Marketing Planning & Consulting
- Access to exclusive downloads & worksheets
- 1-on-1 Social Media Content Coaching
- Editorial Calendar Planning
- Webinars & Conference Calls
- Discounts on Graphic & Web Design

Pick the membership level that is right for you and Use the Coupon Code **SocialMediaGPS** to obtain a 50% discount on your first month of membership.